ANALYZING THE REAL ESTATE (REGULATION AND DEVELOPMENT) ACT, 2016

AUTHORS

Amit K Kashyap

Director, Centre for Corporate Law Studies,

Asst. Prof. of Law, Institute of Law, Nirma University, Ahmedabad, India

Sounak Chakraborty

Student Research Fellow, Centre for Corporate Law Studies, Institute of Law, Nirma University, Ahmedabad, India

Copyright © 2018 Amit K Kashyap & Sounak Chakraborty

All rights reserved.

ISBN: 1987669711
ISBN-13: 978-1987669718

Preface

The Real Estate market, being one of the most significant markets in a developing economy like India, has been one of the most neglected markets in terms of any regulatory aspect. The Real Estate sector in spite of being one of the most rapidly developing sectors and one which contributed heavily in both infrastructural as well as economic development of India lacked any kind of supervision. The sector was being governed through a plethora of confusing legislation which ultimately provided very little recourse to the parties affected from the transactions happening in this sector. Most importantly, the consumers in the Real Estate sector were perhaps the worst affected due to the lack of recourse they had against developers of real estate projects in case of any default in relation to the project construction.

In this report, we analyze the Real Estate (Regulation and Development) Act, 2016 in try to specifically point out the lacunas existing in the Act. In order to conduct a fair analysis we first provide an outlook of the Real Estate market existing in India, followed by the problems existing in the market prior to the enforcement of this Act. We also provide a brief perspective of Real Estate regulations existing in some of the world's leading economies. Thereafter we look at the complex legal framework existing before the Act came into force and how the legislation finally enforced the Act.

The Real Estate (Regulation and Development) Act, 2016 had its inception as a bill in the Union Cabinet way back in 2013. The Act finally came into effect almost 5 years later in 2017. Thus, it is of great importance to check how fruitful the 5 year long wait has been for the Real Estate sector.

Amit K Kashyap

SNG & PARTNERS
Advocates & Solicitors

Foreword

The real estate sector in India had always lacked statutory intervention, leading to unscrupulous and fraudulent practices taking place in rampant across the sector. The promulgation of the Real Estate (Regulation and Development) Act, 2016 ("the Act") was thus a noble attempt to regulate the transactions in the real estate sector. The Act further empowered the States to frame their own rules regarding the sector. The Act largely tries to focus on preserving the rights of the buyers of properties, an aspect which was rather neglected earlier.

The Centre for Corporate Research & Studies, Institute of Law, Nirma University has chosen a rather challenging task of analysing the Act. Furthermore, they have discussed the aspects of the rules framed by the state of Gujarat under the Act. They have conducted a detailed a research highlighting the problems and prospects and have explained the legal intricacies involved under the Act in a very lucid manner. The policy paper has been structured in a manner which enables the reader to understand the Act in a step by step manner. The policy paper discusses both the background as well as the future implications of the Act, thus allowing the reader to complement the laws involved with the practical scenarios existing in the real estate market.

The policy paper is a must read for students of law; practicing advocates and any person involved in the real estate sector. My best wishes to the Centre of Corporate Research & Studies and the authors involved in the research and preparation of this paper. I congratulate the Centre for future research endeavours.

New Delhi
Date: 06.07.2018

Amit Aggarwal
Partner & Head of Corporate Practice
SNG & Partners

Contents

1. Acknowledgements --- 1
2. Methodology -- 2
3. Executive Summary --- 3
4. List of Abbreviations --- 4
5. Brief Overview -- 5
6. Real Estate Market Analysis -- 15
7. Issues in the Real Estate market before the Act --------------------------- 16
8. Global Perspective -- 17
9. Lacunas in earlier laws --- 18
10. Legislative history of the Real Estate (Regulation and Development) Act - 19
11. Analyzing the Real Estate (Regulation and Development) Act, 2016 ------- 20
    - 11.1 Applicability of the Act -- 20
    - 11.2 Authorities under the Act --- 20
    - 11.3 Registration with Authority --- 21
    - 11.4 Defining "Carpet Area" -- 21
    - 11.5 Disclosure by Promoters -- 22
    - 11.6 Separate Account --- 23
    - 11.7 Defining "Engineer" -- 23
    - 11.8 Penal Provisions -- 23
12. GUJRERA --- 25
13. Concluding Remarks --- 27
14. References -- 28
15. Annexures -- 30

Acknowledgements

We are thankful to Prof. Dr. Purvi Pokhariyal, Director & Dean, Institute of Law, Nirma University for giving us the opportunity to conduct this exercise. We would also like to thank Mr. Paresh R. Jani, Solicitor and Advocate, High Court of Gujarat for his constant support and for sharing his invaluable knowledge which immensely helped us in preparing this paper.

Research Methodology

This research report has been created by following an analytical research methodology. The researchers have collected facts and information available through publications and in electronic form. Thereafter the collected information has been synthesized and analyzed in order to critically evaluate the Real Estate (Regulation and Development) Act, 2016. The primary sources relied upon by the researchers were statutes, reports provided by Ministry of Urban Development, Government of India and analysis and research documents of experts of real estate industry like Grant Thornton, FICCI, Cushman & Wakefield and JLL. The researchers also relied upon print and electronic media.

List of Abbreviations

1. Act – The Real Estate (Regulation and Development) Act, 2016
2. Authority – Real Estate Regulatory Authority
3. DDT - Dividend Distribution Tax;
4. FICCI – Federation of Indian Chambers of Commerce and Industry
5. GST - Goods and Service Tax
6. GUJRERA – Gujarat Real Estate Regulatory Authority
7. IAS – Indian Administrative Service
8. NHB – National Housing Bank
9. RBI – Reserve Bank of India
10. Sec. – Section
11. UK – The United Kingdom
12. USA – The United States of America
13. USD – United States Dollars

The Real Estate (Regulation and Development) Act, 2016

Brief Overview

- Received assent of the President of India on 25th March, 2016.
- Came into force on 1st May, 2017

Objectives of the Act:

- Regulation & Promotion of Real Estate Sector
- Ensure sale of apartments, projects etc. in an efficient and transparency manner
- Protect interest of consumers in real estate sector
- Establishment of adjudicating mechanism for speedy dispute redressal
- Standardization of sectorial practices and procedures
- Increasing domestic and foreign investment in the real estate sector

Key Terms

Term	Section (Sec.)	Meaning (summarized)
Promoter (Includes both private and public entities)	Sec. 2(zk)	(i) A person who constructs or causes to be constructed a building or converts an existing building into apartments, for selling all or some of the apartments; or (ii) A person who develops land into a project for; or iii) Any development authority or any other public body in respect of Allottees of— (a) buildings or apartments constructed by such authority; or (b) plots owned by such authority or body or placed at their disposal by the Government, for selling the

		apartments or plots; or
		(iv) State level co-operative housing finance society and a primary co-operative housing society which constructs apartments or buildings for its Members; or
		(v) Any other person who acts himself as a builder, coloniser, contractor, developer, estate developer etc.; or
		(vi) Such other person who constructs any building or apartment for sale to the general public.
Real Estate Project or Project	Sec. 2(zn) & (zj)	Any development or building of a building, or converting any building into apartments, or development of land into plots or apartments, for selling of the apartments or plots or building.
Carpet Area	Sec. 2(k)	Net usable floor area of an apartment, excluding area covered by external walls, including internal partition of the apartment.
Allottee(s)	Sec. 2(d)	The person to whom a plot, apartment or building has been allotted, sold or transferred by the Promoter.
Apartment	Sec. 2(e)	Block, chamber, dwelling unit, flat, office, showroom, shop, godown, premises, unit etc. i.e. a separate and self-contained part of any property, including 1 or more rooms or enclosed spaces, located on 1 or more floors or any part thereof, in a building or on a plot of land, used or to be used for any residential or commercial use or for any business, occupation, profession or trade, or for any other use ancillary thereto.

Registration of Project

- **Registration (Sec. 3)** :
  - Prior to advertisement, marketing, booking, sale, offer for sale etc.
  - Phase wise Registration (*Explanation* to Sec. 3) – (**Phase** – Rule 2 (p) of Registration Rules)

- **Exemption from Registration**:
  - Project with upto 500 sq. mtrs. land or the number of apartments proposed is not more than 8 (inclusive of all phases).
  - Where completion certificate were obtained prior to 1st May, 2017.

- **Requirements for Registration (Disclosures) (Sec. 4)**:
  - Details of Promoter
  - Details of past projects (both complete and ongoing) - launched in past 5 years with status
  - Details of project including proposed and sanctioned plans with the copies of approvals, information relating to FSI/TDR, number, type and carpet area of apartments, garage, car-parking, real estate agents, contractors, architects, engineers etc.
  - Title report
  - Copies of Development/Collaboration Agreement,
  - Details of Encumbrances, proceedings etc.
  - Updates in relation to the sanctions, bookings, status (**Sec-11**)
  - Completion Date (Extension in case of *Force Majeure* and Reasonable circumstances (Sec 6))

- **Deemed registration** if Authority does not reply within 30 days. (**Sec. 5(2)**)

Separate Account

- 70% of the amount realised from allottees to be deposited in a separate account with scheduled bank (**Sec. 4(2)(l)(D)**)

- To cover cost of construction and land cost

- 3 Certificates for withdrawal:

    ➢ Engineer

    ➢ Architect

    ➢ Chartered Accountant

Revocation of registration

- Revocation by the Authority (**Sec. 7**):

- On receipt of complaint or *suo motu or* recommendation of competent authority

- Grounds for revocation:

    ➢ Default by Promoter in doing anything as required by the Act, rules or regulations by the Promoter,

    ➢ Violation of terms of approvals provided by competent authority,

    ➢ Promoter's involvement in unfair practice or irregularities

- 30 day notice to be given to Promoter

Registration for Real Estate Agents

- Shall not facilitate any sale or purchase without registration.

- Shall not facilitate the sale of any unregistered plot, apartment or building. (**Sec. 9**)

- Promoter to disclose names and addresses of Real Estate Agents for proposed projects. (**Sec. 4(2)(j)**)

Compensation

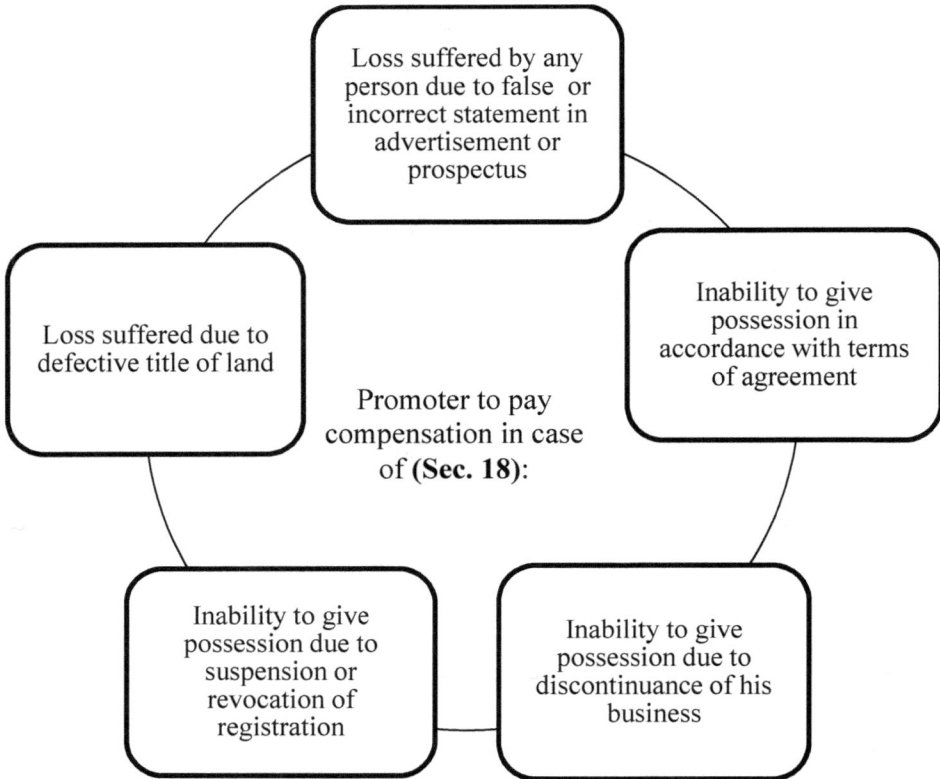

- If allottee wants to withdraw from proposed project, Promoter shall return his entire investment amount with interest and compensation.

- If allottee does not want to withdraw, Promoter shall pay interest for every month till project is handed over.

Requirement of consent

- **Prior consent** of 2/3rd allottees required for :

  - Making any addition or alteration to the plans including common areas (**Sec. 14(2)(ii)**) (Minor additions and alterations permitted)

  - Transferring or assigning majority rights to third party by the Promoter. (**Sec. 15**)

Requirement of Insurance

- Promoter shall obtain insurances in respect of (**Sec 16**):
    - Title of land and building
    - Construction of the project
    - Any other insurance notified by State Government

Conveyance Transfer of title

Application for registration of association within three months from the date when 51% of the allottees have booked their apartments. (**Section 17**)

<u>**Period of conveyance of title**</u>:

S. No.	Project Type	Time
1	Plot	3 months from Allottees paying full consideration
2	Single Building	3 months from issue of Occupation Certificate or 51% of the Allottees paying full consideration
3	Layout	**Building/wing in layout**- 1 month from registration of association/ 3 months from date of issue of Occupation Certificate **Entire layout** - 3 months from the constitution of the Apex Body / issuance of Occupation Certificate to the last building/wing in the layout, whichever is earlier.

Powers of Authority

- Powers of the Authority include:

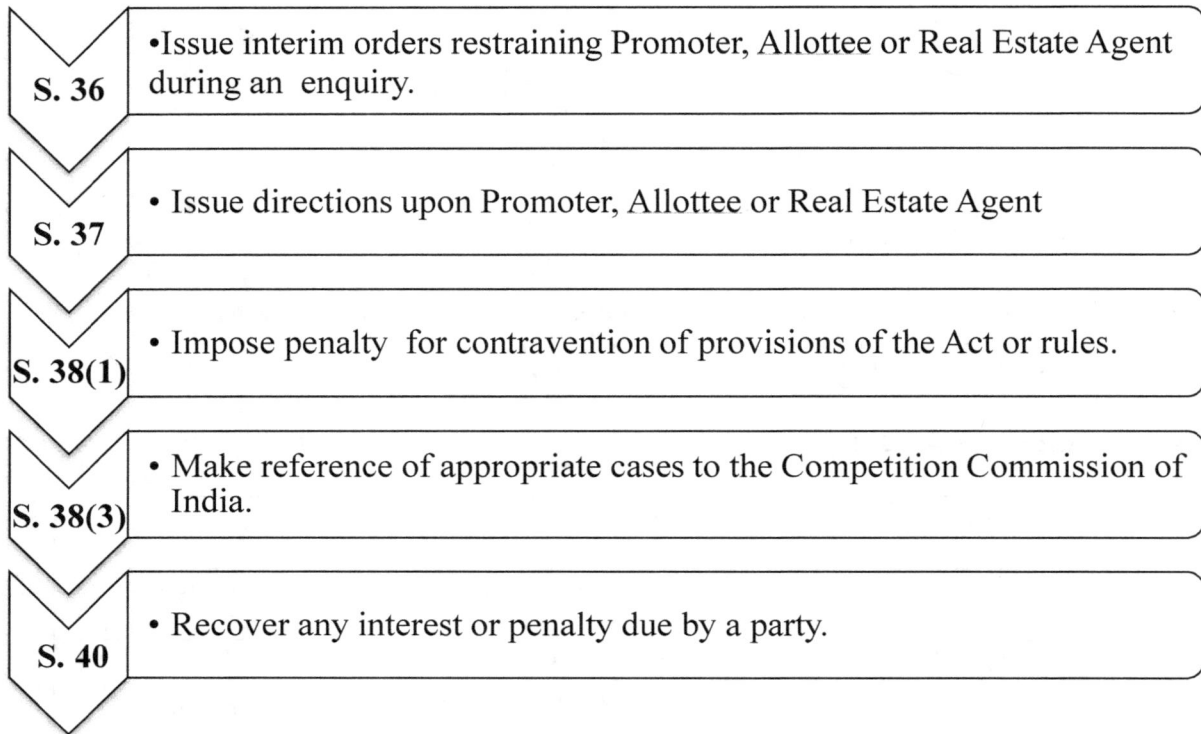

- Authority has power to regulate its own procedures (**Sec. 38(2)**)
- Authority may rectify any order within 2 years of making such order if brought to its notice by the parties. (**Sec. 39**)

Appeal

- Who can file an appeal (**Sec. 44(1)**) :
    - Appropriate Government; or
    - Competent authority; or
    - Any aggrieved person

- Appeal to be filed with the Appellate Tribunal within 60 (sixty) days of receiving the order from the Authority. (**Sec. 44(2)**)

- Appellate Tribunal may entertain any appeal after the expiry of 60 (sixty) days if it is satisfied that there was sufficient cause for not filing within the aforesaid period.

Penalties for Promoters

Offence	Penalty	Relevant Section
Advertise, market, book, sell, offer for sale etc. without registration of project (Contravention of Sec. 3)	Upto 10% of the estimated project	Sec. 59(1)
Continuing violation of Sec. 3	Imprisonment up to 3 (three) years, or a fine which may extend up to further 10% or both	Sec. 59(2)
Providing any false information on RERA's website	Upto 5% of the project cost.	Sec. 60
Contravention of any other provision of Act or rules	up to 5% of the estimated project cost	Sec. 61
Failure to comply with any of the orders or directions of the RERA	Penalty for every day during which such default continues, cumulatively extending up to 5%, of the estimated project cost.	Sec. 63
Failure to comply with any order of the Appellate Tribunal	Imprisonment for a term up to 3 (three) years or fine for every day during which such default continues, which may cumulatively extend up to 10% of the estimated project cost, or both	Sec. 64

Penalties for Allottees:

Offence	Penalty	Relevant Section
Failure to comply with any of the orders, decisions or directions of the Authority	Upto 5% of the plot, apartment or building cost.	Sec. 67
Failure to comply with any of the orders or directions of the Appellate Tribunal	Imprisonment for a term up to 1(one) year or with fine for every day during which such default continues, which may cumulatively extend up to 10% of the plot, apartment or building cost.	Sec. 68

Penalties for Companies:

- Every person who at the time when the offence was committed was responsible for the conduct of the business of the company shall be deemed to be guilty of the offence. (**Sec. 69(1)**)

- If it is proved that an offence has been committed with the consent of, or due to any neglect on the part of any director, manager, secretary or other officer of the company, such person shall be deemed to be guilty of that offence .(**Sec. 69(2)**)

Jurisdiction

- Civil courts have no jurisdiction to entertain any suit or proceeding in respect of any matter which RERA or the Appellate Tribunal is empowered to determine. (**Sec. 79**)

- Competent Courts: No court inferior to a Metropolitan Magistrate or a Judicial Magistrate of the First Class shall try any offence punishable under the Act. **Sec. 80(2)**)

REAL ESTATE MARKET ANALYSIS

The real estate market in India which was worth USD 126 billion in 2015, is expected to reach USD 180 billion by the year 2020.[1] The rising income, rapid urbanization, increase in population are the major reasons which would be responsible for such a rise. Till September, 2017 investments through private equity in the real estate sector in India has exceeded USD 3.2 billion and is expected to rise up to USD 4 billion by the end of 2017.[2] The Government of India has played a major role in the development of the real estate sector through adopting development measures like the 100 Smart City Project and allowing Foreign Direct Investment (FDI) in township and settlement development projects of up to 100%. Further, different policy measures adopted by the Government of India in recent times have had a great impact on the real estate sector. These measures include the introduction of the Benami Transactions (Prohibition) Amendment Act, 2016; interest subsidy to home buyers; change in arbitration laws; Dividend Distribution Tax (DDT) exemption; Goods and Service Tax (GST), and most importantly, the introduction of the Real Estate (Regulation and Development) Act, 2016 (the Act).

Another significant thrust to the real estate sector has been provided by the Government's 'Housing for All' agenda, through which the Government expects to build 20 million affordable homes across India. In order to accomplish this project, the Government in September 2017 came up with Public Private Partnership Models for affordable housing in association with the National Housing Bank (NHB) which will be extending credit facilities to different economic sectors to afford real estate.[3]

Decreased home loan rates are another factor for the growth of the real estate sector. Till 2016 home loan rates were recorded to be around 9.5% per annum, which have now reduced to around 8.4% following RBI's revised lending rates. This has enabled people to easily afford homes and the low EMI costs have resulted in very low differences in costs of renting and owing a house.[4]

---

[1] *Indian Real Estate Industry Analysis*, Indian Brand Equity Foundation (IBEF), https://www.ibef.org/industry/indian-real-estate-industry-analysis-presentation (last updated - October, 2017)
[2] Ibid.
[3] *Public Private Partnership Models for Affordable Housing*, September 2017, Ministry of Housing and Urban Affairs, Government of India, Available at:
http://moud.gov.in/upload/uploadfiles/files/PPP%20Models%20for%20Affordable%20Housing.pdf
[4] *Will 2018 be a good time to invest in real estate?*, Kanika Gupta Shori, Moneycontrol.com, http://www.moneycontrol.com/news/business/personal-finance-business/will-2018-be-a-good-time to-invest-in-real-estate-2448831.html

Issues in the Real Estate market before the Act

Real Estate "includes the land and anything fixed, immovable, or permanently attached to it such as buildings, walls, fixtures, improvements, roads, trees, shrubs, fences, sewers, structures, and utility systems."[5] As per the General Clauses Act, 1897[6], "immovable property" includes "land, benefits to arises out of land, and things attached to the earth, or permanently fastened to anything attached to the earth", and the Transfer of Property Act, 1882[7] states that "immovable property" does not include "standing timber, growing crops or grass." Thus there was no conclusive definition of "real estate", nor any legislation to deal with this sector in India.

The Annual Report (2013-14) of the Ministry of Urban Development stated that the supply of land and housing has not been enough to meet the requirements of the increasing urban population in India.[8] This imbalance in demand in supply led to the growth of arbitrary practices for generating profits by exploiting consumers and also resulted in the emergence and uncontrolled growth of middle-men or agents in the real estate sector. Also, in case of defaults in providing homes to consumers or charging arbitrarily for real estate projects, the builder of developer (Promoter) of a project would hardly have any legal liabilities.

The main objectives for introduction of the Act include regulation and promotion of the real estate sector, protect the interest of consumers in the real estate sector, provide a transparent mechanism for flow of information related to real estate projects between Promoters and consumers, establish a dispute redressal mechanism and an appellate authority for resolving disputes relating to the Act and provide speedy adjudication of such disputes.

Global Perspective

Real Estate market plays a critical role in the economic and infrastructure development of any country. However, the Real Estate market is regulated across countries in very diverse manners. Here we look into the regulatory framework of some of the most economically developed nations[9]:

---

[5] Black's Law Dictionary (2nd Ed.)
[6] Section 2(26), General Clauses Act, 1897.
[7] Section 3, Transfer of Property Act, 1882
[8] Annual Report(2013-2014), Ministry of Urban Development,
Available at: http://moud.gov.in/pdf/582d95bfb0169Annual%20Report%20English%202013-14.pdf
[9] *Real Estate Regulation Act, 2016 (RERA) - Are we ready?* ; Grant Thornton & FICCI, 2016,
Available at: http://www.grantthornton.in/globalassets/ 1.-member-firms/india/assets/pdfs/ real_estate_regulation-act.pdf

United States of America (USA): In USA, real estate is regulated through multiple regulatory bodies. The regulatory bodies are empowered on the basis of different ownership and usage of real estate. The Department of Housing and Urban Development has set rules under the Real Estate Settlement Procedures Act in order to protect the interest of consumers of residential properties. The rights and duties of the developer of a real estate project and the consumer are dealt through the contract between the parties and in case of any violation regarding the terms of the contract, the party can be sued for breach of contract. There is no statute which creates any obligation on the developer or the consumer in relation to real estate projects.

The United Kingdom (UK): There is no regulatory authority to regulate the real estate sector. The Financial Services Authority, a part of the Bank of England regulates only the investments made in the real estate sector. However, in order to restrict false and misleading statements in real estate matters, the Property Misdescriptions Act, 1991 prohibits such practices.

China: China introduced a regulation for the real estate market in 2010. The State Department of Real Estate "New State 10" is a regulation which empowers local governments to control real estate prices. China, like India is aiming to provide affordable housing to promote social development. The regulations allow the developer a benefit of 2-3% changes in the total area of the property in respect to the area stipulated in the sales agreement. In cases where the developer grossly violates the sales agreement, the consumer has recourse to claim a refund from the developer.

Singapore: The government controls land ownership and planning. Properties for housing are regulated by the Housing Development Board, while properties for industrial purposes are regulated by the Jurong Town Corporation. The law provides recourse in the form of compensation in case of any deviation from the sales agreement in relation to possession or allotment date.

Lacunas in earlier laws

The real estate regime, lacking a uniform legislation was earlier governed through a plethora of different laws. The Consumer Protection Act, 1986 initially did not include home buyers under the definition of 'consumers' In 1993, 'housing and construction' was included within the definition of "service" under the Consumer Protection Act.[10] However, in spite of including home buyers within the definition of "consumers", the consumers still faced exploitation. The Consumer Protection Act lacked the teeth to take any punitive measures against the Promoters. There was no standardization of the measures being taken in such cases and due to the large number of consumer disputes before the forum there was an urgent need of a dedicated forum to deal with such cases.

The Act states that any consumer whose case relates to Sections 12, 14, 18 or 19 of the Act, with the permission of the Consumer Disputes Redressal Forum, Consumer Disputes Redressal Commission or National Consumer Redressal Commission, before whom his complaint is lying, may with the permission of such Forum or Commission withdraw his complaint and file an application under the Act before the adjudicating officer appointed under the Act. Thus, the option before a consumer to take his case before the Consumer Forum is not exhausted by commencement of the Act.

Before this Act came into force, the real estate sector was largely governed by state legislations like Town and Country Planning Acts and Apartment Ownership Acts, which resulted in no uniformity across states in India and every state had different requirements in forms of approvals and permissions for real estate related transactions.

---

[10] Consumer Protection (Amendment) Act, (1993)

Legislative history of the Real Estate (Regulation and Development) Act, 2016

The Real Estate (Regulation and Development) Bill (the Bill) was introduced in the year 2013. The Union Cabinet of India in 2015 approved 20 major amendments to this Bill. Thereafter, the Bill was referred to a Select Committee of Rajya Sabha consisting of 21 members, including chairperson to the committee Shri Anil M. Dave. The Select Committee came out with its report in July, 2015. The Bill finally received approval from Rajya Sabha on 10th March, 2015 and thereafter on 15th March, 2015 received approval from Lok Sabha. It received assent of the President of India on 25th March, 2016.

Analyzing the Real Estate (Regulation and Development) Act, 2016

Applicability of the Act

The Act is Applicable on real estate projects, having a proposed area of land for development which measures more than 500 sq. meters, or having more than a total of 8 units, inclusive of all phases. The Act is applicable on both residential and commercial real estate projects. The Appropriate Government, which as per the Act includes State, Union Territory and Central Governments have been given the authority to reduce this limit o which the Act will be applicable.

Authorities under the Act

The Act stipulates the establishments of three entities, two at state level and one at central level.

A **Real Estate Regulatory Authority** (Authority) is to be established in each State and Union Territory which shall consist of one Chairperson and at-least two whole-time members. It is the nodal agency which will be regulating and developing the real estate sector in the concerned State or Union Territory. The Authority is also empowered to protect the interest of consumers and is the adjudicating authority in matters relating to violation of the provisions of the Act; proving compensation to parties; holding enquiry under the provisions of the Act. The adjudicatory functions of the Authority shall be performed by one or more judicial officers, who are present or retired District Judges appointed by the Authority.[11]

The Act there after talks of setting up a **Real Estate Appellate Tribunal** (Appellate Tribunal)[12] which shall be the appellate adjudicatory authority in matters related to the Act. The Appellate Tribunal is composed of one judicial and one administrative member. There is a limitation of 60 days from the date of order of the Authority, within which the appeal before the Appellate Tribunal shall be filed.

---

[11] Section 71 of the Act
[12] Section 43 of the Act.

The third important entity required to be set up under the Act is the **Central Advisory Council** (Council).[13] The Council is an authority set up by the Central Government with the Home Minister being the *ex officio* chairperson, which would evaluate and advise the Central Government on how to effectively implement the Act and develop the laws under the Act.

Registration with Authority

The Act stipulates that Promoters, in order to be able to advertise, market, book, sell or offer for sale their projects, have to first register the Real Estate Project with the Authority.[14] Further, the Act also stipulates that all Real Estate Agents (Agents) who facilitate the sale or purchase of projects also have to register themselves with the Authority.[15] The Authority shall provide the registration to Agents on a periodic basis and the registration has to renewed after the stipulated time as determined by the Authority.[16]

There exists a lacuna in relation to the effective control of the Authority over Agents. As per the Act, only the Agents who is involved in the sale or purchase of a "real estate project" would be deemed to be an Agent. This clearly enables all the real estate brokers existing in the secondary market free from the ambit of the Act. Also, the Act does not provide for any minimum qualification or criteria required to be able to be appointed as an Agent. This may create an issue in cases of resale of properties and in cases where the apartment is being owned by the Promoter personally.

Defining "Carpet Area"

For the first time the term "carpet area" has been defined in a statute and the Pormoterhas to disclose the carpet area of the project at the time of registration with the Authority. Earlier Promoters used different words like "built-up area"; "super-built area" etc. at their own convenience to define the area of the project. Carpet area has been defined as the "net usable floor area of an apartment, excluding the area covered by the external walls, areas underservice shafts, exclusive balcony or verandah area and exclusive open terrace area, but includes the area covered by the internal partition of the apartment". The definition cannot

---
[13] Section 41 of the Act.
[14] Section 3 of the Act.
[15] Section 9 of the Act
[16] Section 9(6) of the Act.

be said to be a simple one, as it would be extremely difficult for the consumer to measure and understand the area covered by internal walls. Also, the non-inclusion of exclusive balcony or verandah will give rise to a situation wherein the Promoter may demand to sell such balcony or verandah or terrace separately from the apartment and may charge additionally for that.

Disclosure by Promoters

The Promoter has to mandatorily register the project with the Authority. The Authority will provide a registration number to the Promoters within thirty days of receiving the application along with a login-id for accessing the website of the Authority to enter details regarding the project.[17] The details to be provided by the Promoter include details of his enterprise including name, registered address and type of the enterprise; details of the projects launched by him in the last five years along with their current status of completion; details of any delay in completion; details of pending litigation; authenticated copy of commencement; details of the Agent, architect, engineer etc. All these details would be available to the public by accessing the website of the Authority.

There is an urgent requirement to include the submission of various safety approvals like Fire Safety Certificate and approvals in relation to structural safety and earthquake safety measures in earthquake prone zones. The inclusion of the obligation on the Promoter to provide the safety certificates would guarantee both increase in the allottee's confidence on the project and make the Promoter further responsible.

Separate Account

The Promoter has been restricted to accept only an amount upto 10% of the cost of the apartment, plot or building without entering into an agreement for sale and without registering such agreement.[18] Further, 70% of the amounts realised from the allotees of the Project has to be deposited in a separate account maintained with a scheduled bank by the Promoter.[19] The money deposited in the separate account has to be utilized exclusively for

---

[17] Section 5(1)(a) of the Act.
[18] Section 13(1) of the Act.
[19] Section 4(1)(D) of the Act.

covering the construction cost of the projects. Also, three certificates from an engineer, architect and chartered accountant respectively are required to make any withdrawal by the Promoter from this account. Also, the account has to be audited each year and the Promoter has to provide statements of accounts to verify that the proceeds had been utilized towards construction costs.

Defining "Engineer"

The term "engineer" under the Act has been defined as a person who "possesses a bachelor's degree or equivalent from an institution recognised by the All India Council of Technical Education University or any institution recognised under a law". This severely restricts the ambit of the term as in India there are multiple engineers involved in the construction of real estate projects are diploma holders and most of the times it is them who visit the site daily and supervise the construction work. The definition should include diploma holders in engineering as "engineers" in order respect the practices of the real estate market and avoid degree holders issuing false certificates in lieu of benefits.

Penal Provisions

The Act provides penalties for contravention of the provisions of the Act by Promoters, Agents and allottees[20]. The allottees face penalties when they contravene the orders or directions of the Authority or Appellate Tribunal. Further, the Act states that when an offence under the Act is committed by a company, each person in charge at the time of commission of the offence would be deemed to be guilty.[21]

---

[20] Chapter VIII o the Act.
[21] Section 69 of the Act.

Gujarat Real Estate Regulatory Authority (GUJRERA)

On 8th March, 2017 the Government of Gujarat established the Gujarat Real Estate Regulatory Authority (GUJRERA) under the Real Estate (Regulation and Development) Act, 2016.

Dr. Manjula Subramaniam IAS (Retd.) has been appointed as the Chairman of the GUJRERA along with two permanent members and secretary.

The Gujarat Real Estate Authority has actively developed its official website (*https://gujrera.gujarat.gov.in*) which has provided Promoters an easy platform for both Promoters and Agents to register themselves. The website provides the list of registered projects and registered Agents and further provides a list of defaulters which can be accessed by the public. The website provides all the requisite forms including the templates of the certificates required for withdrawal from the separate account.

The GUJRERA has formulated three rules under the Act till October, 2017. These rules are:

1. Gujarat Real Estate (Regulation and Development) (General) Rules, 2017
2. Gujarat Real Estate (Regulation and Development) (Matters Relating to the Real Estate Regulatory Authority) Rules, 2016
3. Gujarat Real Estate (Regulation and Development) (Matters Relating to the Gujarat Real Estate Appellate Tribunal) Rules, 2016

Under the General Rules, the information and documents required to be furnished and disclosures to be made by the Promoter for registration of the real estate project along with the requisite fee for registration have been stipulated.[22]

The General Rules also contain the rules governing Agents[23]. Further, it stipulates the rate of interest payable by Promoters and allottees and timelines for refund.

Chapter VI of the General Rules deals with Offences and Penalties and the amount for compounding offences under the Act have been laid down in the following manner[24]:

Offence	Money to be paid for compounding the offence

---

[22] Rule 3 of General Rules
[23] Chapter III of General Rules
[24] Rule 19 of General Rules

Imprisonment under sub section (2) of Sec. 59	5% of the estimated cost of project
Imprisonment under Sec. 64	5% of the estimated cost of the project
Imprisonment under Sec. 66	5% of the estimated cost of the plot, apartment or building, as the case may be, of the real estate project, for which the sale or purchase has been facilitated
Imprisonment under Sec. 68	5% of the estimated cost of the plot, apartment or building, as the case may be

The General Rules provide the model forms of agreement to be entered between Promoter and allottee along with format of application of registration of projects; application of registration of Agents and application for extension of registration of project.

The Real Estate Regulatory Authority Rules states the manner of selection of Chairperson and members of the Authority and their salary and service conditions. The rules further lay down the powers and duties of the Authority. The rules also lay down the manner of filing complaints before the Authority and the manner in which inquiry should be held by the officer.

The Appellate Tribunal Rules pertain to the form of filing appeal before the Appellate Tribunal. Further, it states the manner of selection of members for the Appellate Tribunal. The Government of Gujarat is yet to from the Appellate Tribunal.

Concluding Remarks

With a population of 1.33 billion people and total area of mere 3.3 million sq. km, land is perhaps one of the most scarce resources in India. The real estate sector in India is constantly expanding and the long wait for legislation to regulate this sector finally ended with the enactment of the Real Estate (Regulation and Development) Act, 2016. The Act aims to both "regulate" and "promote" the real estate sector. This is great significance of this objective of the Act, as it proves that the aim is not only to be a regulatory authority by asserting rights and duties of the involved parties, but also play an active part in promoting and helping to expand the real estate sector. The Act has identified the parties involved i.e. the Promoter, the Agents and the allottees, but has restricted itself in defining them as discussed above thereby creating back doors for the parties unwilling to abide by the law to pass through.

The State Governments have been given the authority to draft their own rules pertaining to the Act. This somehow again dilutes the objective of the Act. In order ensure uniformity, the Central Government should have set the rules which would be applicable on all states, in order to do away with any ambiguity among rules of different states in future. Furthermore, several states including Gujarat are yet to set up the Appellate Tribunal within the state.

Hence, in order to achieve the objectives of the Act, it is required that all State Governments should attempt to set up the complete mechanism of regulatory authorities and appellate tribunals at the earliest.

References

1. Annual Report(2013-2014), Ministry of Urban Development, Government of India,

2. Black's Law Dictionary (2nd Ed.), ISBN 1-886363-10-2 .

3. Consumer Protection (Amendment) Act, (1993)

4. General Clauses Act, 1897.

5. Gujarat Real Estate (Regulation and Development) (General) Rules, 2017

6. Gujarat Real Estate (Regulation and Development) (Matters Relating to the Real Estate Regulatory Authority) Rules, 2016

7. Gujarat Real Estate (Regulation and Development) (Matters Relating to the Gujarat Real Estate Appellate Tribunal) Rules, 2016

8. *Indian Real Estate Industry Analysis*, Indian Brand Equity Foundation (IBEF), https://www.ibef.org/industry/indian-real-estate-industry-analysis-presentation (last updated - October, 2017)

9. Indian Real Estate Sector, Annual Handbook, 2017, Grant Thronton, Available at: http://www.grantthornton.in/globalassets/1.-member-firms/india/assets/pdfs/real_estate_handbook-2017.pdf

10. *Indian Real Estate: The Modi Impact*, JLL, September, 2015, Available at: http://www.ap.jll.com/asia-pacific/en-gb/Research/IndiaPaper-ModiFirstYr-Final.pdf

11. *Public Private Partnership Models for Affordable Housing*, September 2017, Ministry of Housing and Urban Affairs, Government of India, Available at: http://moud.gov.in/upload/uploadfiles/files/PPP%20Models%20for%20Affordable%20Housing.pdf

12. Real Estate (Regulation and Development) Act, 2016 – Altering the course of Indian residential sector, Cushman & Wakefield, June 2017, Available at: http://www.cushmanwakefield.co.in/en-gb/research-and-insight/ 2017/realestateact2016/

13. *Real Estate Regulation Act, 2016 (RERA) - Are we ready?* ; Grant Thornton & FICCI, 2016, Available at: http://www.grantthornton.in/globalassets/ 1.-member-firms/india/assets/pdfs/ real_estate_regulation-act.pdf

14. The Real Estate (Regulation and Development) Act, 2016

15. Transfer of Property Act, 1882

16. *Will 2018 be a good time to invest in real estate?*, Kanika Gupta Shori, Moneycontrol.com, http://www.moneycontrol.com/news/business/personal-finance-business/will-2018-be-a-good-time to-invest-in-real-estate-2448831.html

ABOUT THE AUTHERS

Annexures

THE REAL ESTATE (REGULATION AND DEVELOPMENT) ACT, 2016

ARRANGEMENT OF SECTIONS

CHAPTER I
PRELIMINARY

SECTIONS
1. Short title, extent and commencement.
2. Definitions.

CHAPTER II
REGISTRATION OF REAL ESTATE PROJECT AND REGISTRATION OF REAL ESTATE AGENTS

3. Prior registration of real estate project with Real Estate Regulatory Authority.
4. Application for registration of real estate projects.
5. Grant of registration.
6. Extension of registration.
7. Revocation of registration.
8. Obligation of Authority consequent upon lapse of or on revocation of registration.
9. Registration of real estate agents.
10. Functions of real estate agents.

CHAPTER III
FUNCTIONS AND DUTIES OF PROMOTER

11. Functions and duties of promoter.
12. Obligations of promoter regarding veracity of the advertisement or prospectus.
13. No deposit or advance to be taken by promoter without first entering into agreement for sale.
14. Adherence to sanctioned plans and project specifications by the promoter.
15. Obligations of promoter in case of transfer of a real estate project to a third party.
16. Obligations of promoter regarding insurance of real estate project.
17. Transfer of title.
18. Return of amount and compensation.

CHAPTER IV
RIGHTS AND DUTIES OF ALLOTTEES

19. Rights and duties of allottees.

CHAPTET V
THE REAL ESTATE REGULATORY AUTHORITY

20. Establishment and incorporation of Real Estate Regulatory Authority.
21. Composition of Authority.
22. Qualifications of Chairperson and Members of Authority.
23. Term of office of Chairperson and Members.

SECTIONS

24. Salary and allowances payable to Chairperson and Members.
25. Administrative powers of Chairperson.
26. Removal of Chairperson and Members from office in certain circumstances.
27. Restrictions on Chairperson or Members on employment after cessation of office.
28. Officers and other employees of Authority.
29. Meetings of Authority.
30. Vacancies, etc., not to invalidate proceeding of Authority.
31. Filing of complaints with the Authority or the adjudicating officer.
32. Functions of Authority for promotion of real estate sector.
33. Advocacy and awareness measures.
34. Functions of Authority.
35. Powers of Authority to call for information, conduct investigations.
36. Power to issue interim orders.
37. Powers of Authority to issue directions.
38. Powers of Authority.
39. Rectification of orders.
40. Recovery of interest or penalty or compensation and enforcement of order, etc.

CHAPTER VI
CENTRAL ADVISORY COUNCIL

41. Establishment of Central Advisory Council.
42. Functions of Central Advisory Council.

CHAPTER VII
THE REAL ESTATE APPELLATE TRIBUNAL

43. Establishment of Real Estate Appellate Tribunal.
44. Application for settlement of disputes and appeals to Appellate Tribunal.
45. Composition of Appellate Tribunal.
46. Qualifications for appointment of Chairperson and Members.
47. Term of office of Chairperson and Members.
48. Salary and allowances payable to Chairperson and Members.
49. Removal of Chairperson and Member from office in certain circumstances.
50. Restrictions on Chairperson or Judicial Member or Technical or Administrative Member on employment after cessation of office.
51. Officers and other employees of Appellate Tribunal.
52. Vacancies.
53. Powers of Tribunal.
54. Administrative powers of Chairperson of Appellate Tribunal.
55. Vacancies, etc., not to invalidate proceeding of Appellate Tribunal.
56. Right to legal representation.
57. Orders passed by Appellate Tribunal to be executable as a decree.
58. Appeal to High Court.

CHAPTER VIII
OFFENCES, PENALTIES AND ADJUDICATION

SECTIONS

59. Punishment for nonregistration under section 3.
60. Penalty for contravention of section 4.
61. Penalty for contravention of other provisions of this Act.
62. Penalty for nonregistration and contravention under sections 9 and 10.
63. Penalty for failure to comply with orders of Authority by promoter.
64. Penalty for failure to comply with orders of Appellate Tribunal by promoter.
65. Penalty for failure to comply with orders of Authority by real estate agent.
66. Penalty for failure to comply with orders of Appellate Tribunal by real estate agent.
67. Penalty for failure to comply with orders of Authority by allottee.
68. Penalty for failure to comply with orders of Appellate Tribunal by allottee.
69. Offences by companies.
70. Compounding of offences.
71. Power to adjudicate.
72. Factors to be taken into account by the adjudicating officer.

CHAPTER IX
FINANCE, ACCOUNTS, AUDITS AND REPORTS

73. Grants and loans by Central Government.
74. Grants and loans by State Government.
75. Constitution of Fund.
76. Crediting sums realised by way of penalties to Consolidated Fund of India or State account.
77. Budget, accounts and audit.
78. Annual report.

CHAPTER X
MISCELLANEOUS

79. Bar of jurisdiction.
80. Cognizance of offences.
81. Delegation.
82. Power of appropriate Government to supersede Authority.
83. Powers of appropriate Government to issue directions to Authority and obtain reports and returns.
84. Power of appropriate Government to make rules.
85. Power to make regulations.
86. Laying of rules.
87. Members, etc., to be public servants.
88. Application of other laws not barred.
89. Act to have overriding effect.
90. Protection of action taken in good faith.
91. Power to remove difficulties.
92. Repeal.

THE REAL ESTATE (REGULATION AND DEVELOPMENT) ACT, 2016

ACT NO. 16 OF 2016

[25th March, 2016.]

An Act to establish the Real Estate Regulatory Authority for regulation and promotion of the real estate sector and to ensure sale of plot, apartment or building, as the case may be, or sale of real estate project, in an efficient and transparent manner and to protect the interest of consumers in the real estate sector and to establish an adjudicating mechanism for speedy dispute redressal and also to establish the Appellate Tribunal to hear appeals from the decisions, directions or orders of the Real Estate Regulatory Authority and the adjudicating officer and for matters connected therewith or incidental thereto.

BE it enacted by Parliament in the Sixty-seventh Year of the Republic of India as follows:—

CHAPTER I

PRELIMINARY

1. Short title, extent and commencement.—(*1*) This Act may be called the Real Estate (Regulation and Development) Act, 2016.

(*2*) It extends to the whole of India except the State of Jammu and Kashmir.

(*3*) It shall come into force on such date[1] as the Central Government may, by notification in the Official Gazette, appoint:

Provided that different dates may be appointed for different provisions of this Act and any reference in any such provision to the commencement of this Act shall be construed as a reference to the coming into force of that provision.

2. Definitions.—In this Act, unless the context otherwise requires,—

(*a*) "adjudicating officer" means the adjudicating officer appointed under sub-section (*1*) of section 71;

(*b*) "advertisement" means any document described or issued as advertisement through any medium and includes any notice, circular or other documents or publicity in any form, informing persons about a real estate project, or offering for sale of a plot, building or apartment or inviting persons to purchase in any manner such plot, building or apartment or to make advances or deposits for such purposes;

(*c*) "agreement for sale" means an agreement entered into between the promoter and the allottee;

(*d*) "allottee" in relation to a real estate project, means the person to whom a plot, apartment or building, as the case may be, has been allotted, sold (whether as freehold or leasehold) or otherwise transferred by the promoter, and includes the person who subsequently acquires the said allotment through sale, transfer or otherwise but does not include a person to whom such plot, apartment or building, as the case may be, is given on rent;

(*e*) "apartment" whether called block, chamber, dwelling unit, flat, office, showroom, shop, godown, premises, suit, tenement, unit or by any other name, means a separate and self-contained part of any immovable property, including one or more rooms or enclosed spaces, located on one or more floors or any part thereof, in a building or on a plot of land, used or intended to be used for any residential or commercial use such as residence, office, shop, showroom or godown or for carrying on any business, occupation, profession or trade, or for any other type of use ancillary to the purpose specified;

(*f*) "Appellate Tribunal" means the Real Estate Appellate Tribunal established under section 43;

---

1. 1st May, 2016, *vide* notification No. S.O. 1544(E), (Except ss. 3 to 19, 40, 59 to 70, 79 & 80) dated 26th April, 2016, *see* Gazette of India, Extraordinary, Part II, sec. 3(*ii*).

(*g*) "appropriate Government" means in respect of matters relating to,—

(*i*) the Union territory without Legislature, the Central Government;

(*ii*) the Union territory of Puducherry, the Union territory Government;

(*iii*) the Union territory of Delhi, the Central Ministry of Urban Development;

(*iv*) the State, the State Government;

(*h*) "architect" means a person registered as an architect under the provisions of the Architects Act, 1972 (20 of 1972);

(*i*) "Authority" means the Real Estate Regulatory Authority established under sub-section (*1*) of section 20;

(*j*) "building" includes any structure or erection or part of a structure or erection which is intended to be used for residential, commercial or for the purpose of any business, occupation, profession or trade, or for any other related purposes;

(*k*) "carpet area" means the net usable floor area of an apartment, excluding the area covered by the external walls, areas under services shafts, exclusive balcony or verandah area and exclusive open terrace area, but includes the area covered by the internal partition walls of the apartment.

Explanation.— For the purpose of this clause, the expression "exclusive balcony or verandah area" means the area of the balcony or verandah, as the case may be, which is appurtenant to the net usable floor area of an apartment, meant for the exclusive use of the allottee; and "exclusive open terrace area" means the area of open terrace which is appurtenant to the net usable floor area of an apartment, meant for the exclusive use of the allottee;

(*l*) "Chairperson" means the Chairperson of the Real Estate Regulatory Authority appointed under section 21;

(*m*) "commencement certificate" means the commencement certificate or the building permit or the construction permit, by whatever name called issued by the competent authority to allow or permit the promoter to begin development works on an immovable property, as per the sanctioned plan;

(*n*) "common areas" mean—

(*i*) the entire land for the real estate project or where the project is developed in phases and registration under this Act is sought for a phase, the entire land for that phase;

(*ii*) the stair cases, lifts, staircase and lift lobbies, fire escapes, and common entrances and exits of buildings;

(*iii*) the common basements, terraces, parks, play areas, open parking areas and common storage spaces;

(*iv*) the premises for the lodging of persons employed for the management of the property including accommodation for watch and ward staffs or for the lodging of community service personnel;

(*v*) installations of central services such as electricity, gas, water and sanitation, air-conditioning and incinerating, system for water conservation and renewable energy;

(*vi*) the water tanks, sumps, motors, fans, compressors, ducts and all apparatus connected with installations for common use;

(*vii*) all community and commercial facilities as provided in the real estate project;

(*viii*) all other portion of the project necessary or convenient for its maintenance, safety, etc., and in common use;

(*o*) "company" means a company incorporated and registered under the Companies Act, 2013 (18 of 2013) and includes,—

(*i*) a corporation established by or under any Central Act or State Act;

(*ii*) a development authority or any public authority established by the Government in this behalf under any law for the time being in force;

(*p*) "competent authority" means the local authority or any authority created or established under any law for the time being in force by the appropriate Government which exercises authority over land under its jurisdiction, and has powers to give permission for development of such immovable property;

(*q*) "completion certificate" means the completion certificate, or such other certificate, by whatever name called, issued by the competent authority certifying that the real estate project has been developed according to the sanctioned plan, layout plan and specifications, as approved by the competent authority under the local laws;

(*r*) "day" means the working day, in the concerned State or Union territory, as the case may be, notified by the appropriate Government from time to time;

(*s*) "development" with its grammatical variations and cognate expressions, means carrying out the development of immovable property, engineering or other operations in, on, over or under the land or the making of any material change in any immovable property or land and includes re-development;

(*t*) "development works" means the external development works and internal development works on immovable property;

(*u*) "engineer" means a person who possesses a bachelor's degree or equivalent from an institution recognised by the All India Council of Technical Education or any University or any institution recognised under a law or is registered as an engineer under any law for the time being in force;

(*v*) "estimated cost of real estate project" means the total cost involved in developing the real estate project and includes the land cost, taxes, cess, development and other charges;

(*w*) "external development works" includes roads and road systems landscaping, water supply, sewerage and drainage systems, electricity supply transformer, sub-station, solid waste management and disposal or any other work which may have to be executed in the periphery of, or outside, a project for its benefit, as may be provided under the local laws;

(*x*) "family" includes husband, wife, minor son and unmarried daughter wholly dependent on a person;

(*y*) "garage" means a place within a project having a roof and walls on three sides for parking any vehicle, but does not include an unenclosed or uncovered parking space such as open parking areas;

(*z*) "immovable property" includes land, buildings, rights of ways, lights or any other benefit arising out of land and things attached to the earth or permanently fastened to anything which is attached to the earth, but not standing timber, standing crops or grass;

(*za*) "interest" means the rates of interest payable by the promoter or the allottee, as the case may be.

Explanation.—For the purpose of this clause—

(*i*) the rate of interest chargeable from the allottee by the promoter, in case of default, shall be equal to the rate of interest which the promoter shall be liable to pay the allottee, in case of default;

(*ii*) the interest payable by the promoter to the allottee shall be from the date the promoter received the amount or any part thereof till the date the amount or part thereof and interest thereon is refunded, and the interest payable by the allottee to the promoter shall be from the date the allottee defaults in payment to the promoter till the date it is paid;

(*zb*) "internal development works" means roads, footpaths, water supply, sewers, drains, parks, tree planting, street lighting, provision for community buildings and for treatment and disposal of sewage and sullage water, solid waste management and disposal, water conservation, energy management, fire protection and fire safety requirements, social infrastructure such as education health and other public amenities or any other work in a project for its benefit, as per sanctioned plans;

(*zc*) "local authority" means the Municipal Corporation or Municipality or Panchayats or any other Local Body constituted under any law for the time being in force for providing municipal services or basic services, as the case may be, in respect of areas under its jurisdiction;

(*zd*) "Member" means the member of the Real Estate Regulatory Authority appointed under section 21 and includes the Chairperson;

(*ze*) "notification" means a notification published in the Official Gazette and the expression "notify" shall be construed accordingly;

(*zf*) "occupancy certificate" means the occupancy certificate, or such other certificate, by whatever name called, issued by the competent authority permitting occupation of any building, as provided under local laws, which has provision for civic infrastructure such as water, sanitation and electricity;

(*zg*) "Person" includes,—

(*i*) an individual;

(*ii*) a Hindu undivided family;

(*iii*) a company;

(*iv*) a firm under the Indian Partnership Act, 1932 (9 of 1932) or the Limited Liability Partnership Act, 2008 (6 of 2009), as the case may be;

(*v*) a competent authority;

(*vi*) an association of persons or a body of individuals whether incorporated or not;

(*vii*) a co-operative society registered under any law relating to co-operative societies;

(*viii*) any such other entity as the appropriate Government may, by notification, specify in this behalf;

(*zh*) "planning area" means a planning area or a development area or a local planning area or a regional development plan area, by whatever name called, or any other area specified as such by the appropriate Government or any competent authority and includes any area designated by the appropriate Government or the competent authority to be a planning area for future planned development, under the law relating to Town and Country Planning for the time being in force and as revised from time to time;

(*zi*) "prescribed" means prescribed by rules made under this Act;

(*zj*) "project" means the real estate project as defined in clause (*zn*);

(*zk*) "promoter" means,—

(*i*) a person who constructs or causes to be constructed an independent building or a building consisting of apartments, or converts an existing building or a part thereof into apartments, for the purpose of selling all or some of the apartments to other persons and includes his assignees; or

(*ii*) a person who develops land into a project, whether or not the person also constructs structures on any of the plots, for the purpose of selling to other persons all or some of the plots in the said project, whether with or without structures thereon; or (*iii*) any development authority or any other public body in respect of allottees of—

(*a*) buildings or apartments, as the case may be, constructed by such authority or body on lands owned by them or placed at their disposal by the Government; or

(*b*) plots owned by such authority or body or placed at their disposal by the Government, for the purpose of selling all or some of the apartments or plots; or

(*iv*) an apex State level co-operative housing finance society and a primary co-operative housing society which constructs apartments or buildings for its Members or in respect of the allottees of such apartments or buildings; or

(*v*) any other person who acts himself as a builder, coloniser, contractor, developer, estate developer or by any other name or claims to be acting as the holder of a power of attorney from the owner of the land on which the building or apartment is constructed or plot is developed for sale; or

(*vi*) such other person who constructs any building or apartment for sale to the general public.

Explanation.—For the purposes of this clause, where the person who constructs or converts a building into apartments or develops a plot for sale and the person who sells apartments or plots are different person, both of them shall be deemed to be the promoters and shall be jointly liable as such for the functions and responsibilities specified under this Act or the rules and regulations made thereunder;

(*zl*) "prospectus" means any document described or issued as a prospectus or any notice, circular, or other document offering for sale of any real estate project or inviting any person to make advances or deposits for such purposes;

(*zm*) "real estate agent" means any person, who negotiates or acts on behalf of one person in a transaction of transfer of his plot, apartment or building, as the case may be, in a real estate project, by way of sale, with another person or transfer of plot, apartment or building, as the case may be, of any other person to him and receives remuneration or fees or any other charges for his services whether as a commission or otherwise and includes a person who introduces, through any medium, prospective buyers and sellers to each other for negotiation for sale or purchase of plot, apartment or building, as the case may be, and includes property dealers, brokers, middlemen by whatever name called;

(*zn*) "real estate project" means the development of a building or a building consisting of apartments, or converting an existing building or a part thereof into apartments, or the development of land into plots or apartments, as the case may be, for the purpose of selling all or some of the said apartments or plots or building, as the case may be, and includes the common areas, the development works, all improvements and structures thereon, and all easement, rights and appurtenances belonging thereto;

(*zo*) "regulations" means the regulations made by the Authority under this Act;

(*zp*) "rule" means the rules made under this Act by the appropriate Government;

(*zq*) "sanctioned plan" means the site plan, building plan, service plan, parking and circulation plan, landscape plan, layout plan, zoning plan and such other plan and includes structural designs, if applicable, permissions such as environment permission and such other permissions, which are approved by the competent authority prior to start of a real estate project;

(*zr*) words and expressions used herein but not defined in this Act and defined in any law for the time being in force or in the municipal laws or such other relevant laws of the appropriate Government shall have the same meanings respectively assigned to them in those laws.

CHAPTER II

REGISTRATION OF REAL ESTATE PROJECT AND REGISTRATION OF REAL ESTATE AGENTS

3. Prior registration of real estate project with Real Estate Regulatory Authority.—(*1*) No promoter shall advertise, market, book, sell or offer for sale, or invite persons to purchase in any manner any plot, apartment or building, as the case may be, in any real estate project or part of it, in any planning area, without registering the real estate project with the Real Estate Regulatory Authority established under this Act:

Provided that projects that are ongoing on the date of commencement of this Act and for which the completion certificate has not been issued, the promoter shall make an application to the Authority for registration of the said project within a period of three months from the date of commencement of this Act:

Provided further that if the Authority thinks necessary, in the interest of allottees, for projects which are developed beyond the planning area but with the requisite permission of the local authority, it may, by order, direct the promoter of such project to register with the Authority, and the provisions of this Act or the rules and regulations made thereunder, shall apply to such projects from that stage of registration.

(*2*) Notwithstanding anything contained in sub-section (*1*), no registration of the real estate project shall be required—

(*a*) where the area of land proposed to be developed does not exceed five hundred square meters or the number of apartments proposed to be developed does not exceed eight inclusive of all phases:

Provided that, if the appropriate Government considers it necessary, it may, reduce the threshold below five hundred square meters or eight apartments, as the case may be, inclusive of all phases, for exemption from registration under this Act;

(*b*) where the promoter has received completion certificate for a real estate project prior to commencement of this Act;

(*c*) for the purpose of renovation or repair or re-development which does not involve marketing, advertising selling or new allotment of any apartment, plot or building, as the case may be, under the real estate project.

Explanation.—For the purpose of this section, where the real estate project is to be developed in phases, every such phase shall be considered a stand alone real estate project, and the promoter shall obtain registration under this Act for each phase separately.

4. Application for registration of real estate projects.—(*1*) Every promoter shall make an application to the Authority for registration of the real estate project in such form, manner, within such time and accompanied by such fee as may be [1][prescribed].

(*2*) The promoter shall enclose the following documents along with the application referred to in sub-section (*1*), namely:—

(*a*) a brief details of his enterprise including its name, registered address, type of enterprise (proprietorship, societies, partnership, companies, competent authority), and the particulars of registration, and the names and photographs of the promoter;

(*b*) a brief detail of the projects launched by him, in the past five years, whether already completed or being developed, as the case may be, including the current status of the said projects, any delay in its completion, details of cases pending, details of type of land and payments pending;

(*c*) an authenticated copy of the approvals and commencement certificate from the competent authority obtained in accordance with the laws as may be applicable for the real estate project mentioned in the application, and where the project is proposed to be developed in phases, an authenticated copy of the approvals and commencement certificate from the competent authority for each of such phases;

---

1. Subs. by the Real Estate (Regulation and Development) Removal of Difficulties Order, 2016 [S.O. 3347 (E)], for "specified by the regulations made by the Authority" (w.e.f. 28-10-2016).

(*d*) the sanctioned plan, layout plan and specifications of the proposed project or the phase thereof, and the whole project as sanctioned by the competent authority;

(*e*) the plan of development works to be executed in the proposed project and the proposed facilities to be provided thereof including fire fighting facilities, drinking water facilities, emergency evacuation services, use of renewable energy;

(*f*) the location details of the project, with clear demarcation of land dedicated for the project along with its boundaries including the latitude and longitude of the end points of the project;

(*g*) proforma of the allotment letter, agreement for sale, and the conveyance deed proposed to be signed with the allottees;

(*h*) the number, type and the carpet area of apartments for sale in the project along with the area of the exclusive balcony or verandah areas and the exclusive open terrace areas appurtenant with the apartment, if any;

(*i*) the number and area of garage for sale in the project;

(*j*) the names and addresses of his real estate agents, if any, for the proposed project;

(*k*) the names and addresses of the contractors, architect, structural engineer, if any and other persons concerned with the development of the proposed project;

(*l*) a declaration, supported by an affidavit, which shall be signed by the promoter or any person authorised by the promoter, stating:—

(*A*) that he has a legal title to the land on which the development is proposed along with legally valid documents with authentication of such title, if such land is owned by another person;

(*B*) that the land is free from all encumbrances, or as the case may be details of the encumbrances on such land including any rights, title, interest or name of any party in or over such land along with details;

(*C*) the time period within which he undertakes to complete the project or phase thereof, as the case may be;

(*D*) that seventy per cent. of the amounts realised for the real estate project from the allottees, from time to time, shall be deposited in a separate account to be maintained in a scheduled bank to cover the cost of construction and the land cost and shall be used only for that purpose:

Provided that the promoter shall withdraw the amounts from the separate account, to cover the cost of the project, in proportion to the percentage of completion of the project:

Provided further that the amounts from the separate account shall be withdrawn by the promoter after it is certified by an engineer, an architect and a chartered accountant in practice that the withdrawal is in proportion to the percentage of completion of the project:

Provided also that the promoter shall get his accounts audited within six months after the end of every financial year by a chartered accountant in practice, and shall produce a statement of accounts duly certified and signed by such chartered accountant and it shall be verified during the audit that the amounts collected for a particular project have been utilised for that project and the withdrawal has been in compliance with the proportion to the percentage of completion of the project.

Explanation.—For the purpose of this clause, the term "scheduled bank" means a bank included in the Second Scheduled to the Reserve Bank of India Act, 1934 (2 of 1934);

(*E*) that he shall take all the pending approvals on time, from the competent authorities;

(*F*) that he has furnished such other documents as may be prescribed by the rules or regulations made under this Act; and

(*m*) such other information and documents as may be prescribed.

(*3*) The Authority shall operationalise a web based online system for submitting applications for registration of projects within a period of one year from the date of its establishment.

5. Grant of registration.—(*1*) On receipt of the application under sub-section (*1*) of section 4, the Authority shall within a period of thirty days.

(*a*) grant registration subject to the provisions of this Act and the rules and regulations made thereunder, and provide a registration number, including a Login Id and password to the applicant for accessing the website of the Authority and to create his web page and to fill therein the details of the proposed project; or

(*b*) reject the application for reasons to be recorded in writing, if such application does not conform to the provisions of this Act or the rules or regulations made thereunder:

Provided that no application shall be rejected unless the applicant has been given an opportunity of being heard in the matter.

(*2*) If the Authority fails to grant the registration or reject the application, as the case may be, as provided under sub-section (*1*), the project shall be deemed to have been registered, and the Authority shall within a period of seven days of the expiry of the said period of thirty days specified under sub-section (*1*), provide a registration number and a Login Id and password to the promoter for accessing the website of the Authority and to create his web page and to fill therein the details of the proposed project.

(*3*) The registration granted under this section shall be valid for a period declared by the promoter under sub-clause (*C*) of clause (*l*) of sub-section (*2*) of section 4 for completion of the project or phase thereof, as the case may be.

6. Extension of registration.—The registration granted under section 5 may be extended by the Authority on an application made by the promoter, due to force majeure, in such form and on payment of such fee as may be [1][prescribed]:

Provided that the Authority may in reasonable circumstances, without default on the part of the promoter, based on the facts of each case, and for reasons to be recorded in writing, extend the registration granted to a project for such time as it considers necessary, which shall, in aggregate, not exceed a period of one year:

Provided further that no application for extension of registration shall be rejected unless the applicant has been given an opportunity of being heard in the matter.

Explanation.— For the purpose of this section, the expression "force majeure" shall mean a case of war, flood, drought, fire, cyclone, earthquake or any other calamity caused by nature affecting the regular development of the real estate project.

7. Revocation of registration.—(*1*) The Authority may, on receipt of a complaint or *suo motu* in this behalf or on the recommendation of the competent authority, revoke the registration granted under section 5, after being satisfied that—

(*a*) the promoter makes default in doing anything required by or under this Act or the rules or the regulations made thereunder;

(*b*) the promoter violates any of the terms or conditions of the approval given by the competent authority;

(*c*) the promoter is involved in any kind of unfair practice or irregularities.

Explanation.—For the purposes of this clause, the term "unfair practice means" a practice which, for the purpose of promoting the sale or development of any real estate project adopts any unfair method or unfair or deceptive practice including any of the following practices, namely:—

(*A*) the practice of making any statement, whether in writing or by visible representation which,—

(*i*) falsely represents that the services are of a particular standard or grade;

---

1. Subs. by the Real Estate (Regulation and Development) Removal of Difficulties Order, 2016 [S.O. 3347 (E)], for "specified by regulations made by the Authority" (w.e.f. 28-10-2016).

(*ii*) represents that the promoter has approval or affiliation which such promoter does not have;

(*iii*) makes a false or misleading representation concerning the services;

(*B*) the promoter permits the publication of any advertisement or prospectus whether in any newspaper or otherwise of services that are not intended to be offered;

(*d*) the promoter indulges in any fraudulent practices.

(*2*) The registration granted to the promoter under section 5 shall not be revoked unless the Authority has given to the promoter not less than thirty days notice, in writing, stating the grounds on which it is proposed to revoke the registration, and has considered any cause shown by the promoter within the period of that notice against the proposed revocation.

(*3*) The Authority may, instead of revoking the registration under sub-section (*1*), permit it to remain in force subject to such further terms and conditions as it thinks fit to impose in the interest of the allottees, and any such terms and conditions so imposed shall be binding upon the promoter.

(*4*) The Authority, upon the revocation of the registration,—

(*a*) shall debar the promoter from accessing its website in relation to that project and specify his name in the list of defaulters and display his photograph on its website and also inform the other Real Estate Regulatory Authority in other States and Union territories about such revocation or registration;

(*b*) shall facilitate the remaining development works to be carried out in accordance with the provisions of section 8;

(*c*) shall direct the bank holding the project bank account, specified under sub-clause (*D*) of clause (*l*) of sub-section (*2*) of section 4, to freeze the account, and thereafter take such further necessary actions, including consequent de-freezing of the said account, towards facilitating the remaining development works in accordance with the provisions of section 8;

(*d*) may, to protect the interest of allottees or in the public interest, issue such directions as it may deem necessary.

8. Obligation of Authority consequent upon lapse of or on revocation of registration.—Upon lapse of the registration or on revocation of the registration under this Act, the Authority, may consult the appropriate Government to take such action as it may deem fit including the carrying out of the remaining development works by competent authority or by the association of allottees or in any other manner, as may be determined by the Authority:

Provided that no direction, decision or order of the Authority under this section shall take effect until the expiry of the period of appeal provided under the provisions of this Act:

Provided further that in case of revocation of registration of a project under this Act, the association of allottees shall have the first right of refusal for carrying out of the remaining development works.

9. Registration of real estate agents.—(*1*) No real estate agent shall facilitate the sale or purchase of or act on behalf of any person to facilitate the sale or purchase of any plot, apartment or building, as the case may be, in a real estate project or part of it, being the part of the real estate project registered under section 3, being sold by the promoter in any planning area, without obtaining registration under this section.

(*2*) Every real estate agent shall make an application to the Authority for registration in such form, manner, within such time and accompanied by such fee and documents as may be prescribed.

(*3*) The Authority shall, within such period, in such manner and upon satisfying itself of the fulfilment of such conditions, as may be prescribed—

(*a*) grant a single registration to the real estate agent for the entire State or Union territory, as the case may be;

(*b*) reject the application for reasons to be recorded in writing, if such application does not conform to the provisions of the Act or this rules or regulations made thereunder:

Provided that no application shall be rejected unless the applicant has been given an opportunity of being heard in the matter.

(*4*) Whereon the completion of the period specified under sub-section (*3*), if the applicant does not receive any communication about the deficiencies in his application or the rejection of his application, he shall be deemed to have been registered.

(*5*) Every real estate agent who is registered as per the provisions of this Act or the rules and regulations made thereunder, shall be granted a registration number by the Authority, which shall be quoted by the real estate agent in every sale facilitated by him under this Act.

(*6*) Every registration shall be valid for such period as may be prescribed, and shall be renewable for a period in such manner and on payment of such fee as may be prescribed.

(*7*) Where any real estate agent who has been granted registration under this Act commits breach of any of the conditions thereof or any other terms and conditions specified under this Act or any rules or regulations made thereunder, or where the Authority is satisfied that such registration has been secured by the real estate agent through misrepresentation or fraud, the Authority may, without prejudice to any other provisions under this Act, revoke the registration or suspend the same for such period as it thinks fit:

Provided that no such revocation or suspension shall be made by the Authority unless an opportunity of being heard has been given to the real estate agent.

10. Functions of real estate agents.—Every real estate agent registered under section 9 shall—

(*a*) not facilitate the sale or purchase of any plot, apartment or building, as the case may be, in a real estate project or part of it, being sold by the promoter in any planning area, which is not registered with the Authority;

(*b*) maintain and preserve such books of account, records and documents as may be prescribed;

(*c*) not involve himself in any unfair trade practices, namely:—

(*i*) the practice of making any statement, whether orally or in writing or by visible representation which—

(*A*) falsely represents that the services are of a particular standard or grade;

(*B*) represents that the promoter or himself has approval or affiliation which such promoter or himself does not have;

(*C*) makes a false or misleading representation concerning the services;

(*ii*) permitting the publication of any advertisement whether in any newspaper or otherwise of services that are not intended to be offered.

(*d*) facilitate the possession of all the information and documents, as the allottee, is entitled to, at the time of booking of any plot, apartment or building, as the case may be;

(*e*) discharge such other functions as may be prescribed.

CHAPTER III

FUNCTIONS AND DUTIES OF PROMOTER

11. Functions and duties of promoter.—(*1*) The promoter shall, upon receiving his Login Id and password under clause (*a*) of sub-section (*1*) or under sub-section (*2*) of section 5, as the case may be, create his web page on the website of the Authority and enter all details of the proposed project as provided under sub-section (*2*) of section 4, in all the fields as provided, for public viewing, including—

(*a*) details of the registration granted by the Authority;

(*b*) quarterly up-to-date the list of number and types of apartments or plots, as the case may be, booked;

(*c*) quarterly up-to-date the list of number of garages booked;

(*d*) quarterly up-to-date the list of approvals taken and the approvals which are pending subsequent to commencement certificate;

(*e*) quarterly up-to-date status of the project; and

(*f*) such other information and documents as may be specified by the regulations made by the Authority.

(2) The advertisement or prospectus issued or published by the promoter shall mention prominently the website address of the Authority, wherein all details of the registered project have been entered and include the registration number obtained from the Authority and such other matters incidental thereto.

(3) The promoter, at the time of the booking and issue of allotment letter shall be responsible to make available to the allottee, the following information, namely:—

(*a*) sanctioned plans, layout plans, along with specifications, approved by the competent authority, by display at the site or such other place as may be specified by the regulations made by the Authority;

(*b*) the stage wise time schedule of completion of the project, including the provisions for civic infrastructure like water, sanitation and electricity.

(4) The promoter shall—

(*a*) be responsible for all obligations, responsibilities and functions under the provisions of this Act or the rules and regulations made thereunder or to the allottees as per the agreement for sale, or to the association of allottees, as the case may be, till the conveyance of all the apartments, plots or buildings, as the case may be, to the allottees, or the common areas to the association of allottees or the competent authority, as the case may be:

Provided that the responsibility of the promoter, with respect to the structural defect or any other defect for such period as is referred to in sub-section (3) of section 14, shall continue even after the conveyance deed of all the apartments, plots or buildings, as the case may be, to the allottees are executed.

(*b*) be responsible to obtain the completion certificate or the occupancy certificate, or both, as applicable, from the relevant competent authority as per local laws or other laws for the time being in force and to make it available to the allottees individually or to the association of allottees, as the case may be;

(*c*) be responsible to obtain the lease certificate, where the real estate project is developed on a leasehold land, specifying the period of lease, and certifying that all dues and charges in regard to the leasehold land has been paid, and to make the lease certificate available to the association of allottees;

(*d*) be responsible for providing and maintaining the essential services, on reasonable charges, till the taking over of the maintenance of the project by the association of the allottees;

(*e*) enable the formation of an association or society or co-operative society, as the case may be, of the allottees, or a federation of the same, under the laws applicable:

Provided that in the absence of local laws, the association of allottees, by whatever name called, shall be formed within a period of three months of the majority of allottees having booked their plot or apartment or building, as the case may be, in the project;

(*f*) execute a registered conveyance deed of the apartment, plot or building, as the case may be, in favour of the allottee along with the undivided proportionate title in the common areas to the association of allottees or competent authority, as the case may be, as provided under section 17 of this Act;

(g) pay all outgoings until he transfers the physical possession of the real estate project to the allottee or the associations of allottees, as the case may be, which he has collected from the allottees, for the payment of outgoings (including land cost, ground rent, municipal or other local taxes, charges for water or electricity, maintenance charges, including mortgage loan and interest on mortgages or other encumbrances and such other liabilities payable to competent authorities, banks and financial institutions, which are related to the project):

Provided that where any promoter fails to pay all or any of the outgoings collected by him from the allottees or any liability, mortgage loan and interest thereon before transferring the real estate project to such allottees, or the association of the allottees, as the case may be, the promoter shall continue to be liable, even after the transfer of the property, to pay such outgoings and penal charges, if any, to the authority or person to whom they are payable and be liable for the cost of any legal proceedings which may be taken therefor by such authority or person;

(h) after he executes an agreement for sale for any apartment, plot or building, as the case may be, not mortgage or create a charge on such apartment, plot or building, as the case may be, and if any such mortgage or charge is made or created then notwithstanding anything contained in any other law for the time being in force, it shall not affect the right and interest of the allottee who has taken or agreed to take such apartment, plot or building, as the case may be;

(5) The promoter may cancel the allotment only in terms of the agreement for sale:

Provided that the allottee may approach the Authority for relief, if he is aggrieved by such cancellation and such cancellation is not in accordance with the terms of the agreement for sale, unilateral and without any sufficient cause.

(6) The promoter shall prepare and maintain all such other details as may be specified, from time to time, by regulations made by the Authority.

12. Obligations of promoter regarding veracity of the advertisement or prospectus.—Where any person makes an advance or a deposit on the basis of the information contained in the notice, advertisement or prospectus, or on the basis of any model apartment, plot or building, as the case may be, and sustains any loss or damage by reason of any incorrect, false statement included therein, he shall be compensated by the promoter in the manner as provided under this Act:

Provided that if the person affected by such incorrect, false statement contained in the notice, advertisement or prospectus, or the model apartment, plot or building as the case may be, intends to withdraw from the proposed project, he shall be returned his entire investment along with interest at such rate as may be prescribed and the compensation in the manner provided under this Act.

13. No deposit or advance to be taken by promoter without first entering into agreement for sale. —(1) A promoter shall not accept a sum more than ten per cent. of the cost of the apartment, plot, or building as the case may be, as an advance payment or an application fee, from a person without first entering into a written agreement for sale with such person and register the said agreement for sale, under any law for the time being in force.

(2) The agreement for sale referred to in sub-section (1) shall be in such form as may be prescribed and shall specify the particulars of development of the project including the construction of building and apartments, along with specifications and internal development works and external development works, the dates and the manner by which payments towards the cost of the apartment, plot, or building, as the case may be, are to be made by the allottees and the date on which the possession of the apartment, plot or building is to be handed over, the rates of interest payable by the promoter to the allottee and the allottee to the promoter in case of default, and such other particulars, as may be prescribed.

14. Adherence to sanctioned plans and project specifications by the promoter.—(1) The proposed project shall be developed and completed by the promoter in accordance with the sanctioned plans, layout plans and specifications as approved by the competent authorities.

(2) Notwithstanding anything contained in any law, contract or agreement, after the sanctioned plans, layout plans and specifications and the nature of the fixtures, fittings, amenities and common areas, of the

apartment, plot or building, as the case may be, as approved by the competent authority, are disclosed or furnished to the person who agree to take one or more of the said apartment, plot or building, as the case may be, the promoter shall not make—

(*i*) any additions and alterations in the sanctioned plans, layout plans and specifications and the nature of fixtures, fittings and amenities described therein in respect of the apartment, plot or building, as the case may be, which are agreed to be taken, without the previous consent of that person:

Provided that the promoter may make such minor additions or alterations as may be required by the allottee, or such minor changes or alterations as may be necessary due to architectural and structural reasons duly recommended and verified by an authorised Architect or Engineer after proper declaration and intimation to the allottee.

Explanation.—For the purpose of this clause, "minor additions or alterations" excludes structural change including an addition to the area or change in height, or the removal of part of a building, or any change to the structure, such as the construction or removal or cutting into of any wall or a part of a wall, partition, column, beam, joist, floor including a mezzanine floor or other support, or a change to or closing of any required means of access ingress or egress or a change to the fixtures or equipment, etc.

(*ii*) any other alterations or additions in the sanctioned plans, layout plans and specifications of the buildings or the common areas within the project without the previous written consent of at least two-thirds of the allottees, other than the promoter, who have agreed to take apartments in such building.

Explanation.—For the purpose of this clause, the allottee, irrespective of the number of apartments or plots, as the case may be, booked by him or booked in the name of his family, or in the case of other persons such as companies or firms or any association of individuals, etc., by whatever name called, booked in its name or booked in the name of its associated entities or related enterprises, shall be considered as one allottee only.

(*3*) In case any structural defect or any other defect in workmanship, quality or provision of services or any other obligations of the promoter as per the agreement for sale relating to such development is brought to the notice of the promoter within a period of five years by the allottee from the date of handing over possession, it shall be the duty of the promoter to rectify such defects without further charge, within thirty days, and in the event of promoter's failure to rectify such defects within such time, the aggrieved allottees shall be entitled to receive appropriate compensation in the manner as provided under this Act.

15. Obligations of promoter in case of transfer of a real estate project to a third party.—(*1*) The promoter shall not transfer or assign his majority rights and liabilities in respect of a real estate project to a third party without obtaining prior written consent from two-third allottees, except the promoter, and without the prior written approval of the Authority:

Provided that such transfer or assignment shall not affect the allotment or sale of the apartments, plots or buildings as the case may be, in the real estate project made by the erstwhile promoter.

Explanation.—For the purpose of this sub-section, the allottee, irrespective of the number of apartments or plots, as the case may be, booked by him or booked in the name of his family, or in the case of other persons such as companies or firms or any association of individuals, by whatever name called, booked in its name or booked in the name of its associated entities or related enterprises, shall be considered as one allottee only.

(*2*) On the transfer or assignment being permitted by the allottees and the Authority under sub-section (*1*), the intending promoter shall be required to independently comply with all the pending obligations under the provisions of this Act or the rules and regulations made thereunder, and the pending obligations as per the agreement for sale entered into by the erstwhile promoter with the allottees:

Provided that any transfer or assignment permitted under provisions of this section shall not result in extension of time to the intending promoter to complete the real estate project and he shall be required to comply with all the pending obligations of the erstwhile promoter, and in case of default, such intending promoter shall be liable to the consequences of breach or delay, as the case may be, as provided under this Act or the rules and regulations made thereunder.

16. Obligations of promoter regarding insurance of real estate project.—(*1*) The promoter shall obtain all such insurances as may be notified by the appropriate Government, including but not limited to insurance in respect of —

(*i*) title of the land and building as a part of the real estate project; and

(*ii*) construction of the real estate project.

(*2*) The promoter shall be liable to pay the premium and charges in respect of the insurance specified in sub-section (*1*) and shall pay the same before transferring the insurance to the association of the allottees.

(*3*) The insurance as specified under sub-section (*1*) shall stand transferred to the benefit of the allottee or the association of allottees, as the case may be, at the time of promoter entering into an agreement for sale with the allottee.

(*4*) On formation of the association of the allottees, all documents relating to the insurance specified under sub-section (*1*) shall be handed over to the association of the allottees.

17. Transfer of title.—(*1*) The promoter shall execute a registered conveyance deed in favour of the allottee along with the undivided proportionate title in the common areas to the association of the allottees or the competent authority, as the case may be, and hand over the physical possession of the plot, apartment of building, as the case may be, to the allottees and the common areas to the association of the allottees or the competent authority, as the case may be, in a real estate project, and the other title documents pertaining thereto within specified period as per sanctioned plans as provided under the local laws:

Provided that, in the absence of any local law, conveyance deed in favour of the allottee or the association of the allottees or the competent authority, as the case may be, under this section shall be carried out by the promoter within three months from date of issue of occupancy certificate.

(*2*) After obtaining the occupancy certificate and handing over physical possession to the allottees in terms of sub-section (*1*), it shall be the responsibility of the promoter to handover the necessary documents and plans, including common areas, to the association of the allottees or the competent authority, as the case may be, as per the local laws:

Provided that, in the absence of any local law, the promoter shall handover the necessary documents and plans, including common areas, to the association of the allottees or the competent authority, as the case may be, within thirty days after obtaining the [1][completion] certificate.

18. Return of amount and compensation.—(*1*) If the promoter fails to complete or is unable to give possession of an apartment, plot or building,—

(*a*) in accordance with the terms of the agreement for sale or, as the case may be, duly completed by the date specified therein; or

(*b*) due to discontinuance of his business as a developer on account of suspension or revocation of the registration under this Act or for any other reason,

he shall be liable on demand to the allottees, in case the allottee wishes to withdraw from the project, without prejudice to any other remedy available, to return the amount received by him in respect of that apartment, plot, building, as the case may be, with interest at such rate as may be prescribed in this behalf including compensation in the manner as provided under this Act:

Provided that where an allottee does not intend to withdraw from the project, he shall be paid, by the promoter, interest for every month of delay, till the handing over of the possession, at such rate as may be prescribed.

(*2*) The promoter shall compensate the allottees in case of any loss caused to him due to defective title of the land, on which the project is being developed or has been developed, in the manner as provided

---

1. Subs. by the Real Estate (Regulation and Development) Removal of Difficulties Order, 2016 [S.O. 3347(E), for "occupancy" (w.e.f. 28-10-2016).

under this Act, and the claim for compensation under this subsection shall not be barred by limitation provided under any law for the time being in force.

(*3*) If the promoter fails to discharge any other obligations imposed on him under this Act or the rules or regulations made thereunder or in accordance with the terms and conditions of the agreement for sale, he shall be liable to pay such compensation to the allottees, in the manner as provided under this Act.

CHAPTER IV

RIGHTS AND DUTIES OF ALLOTTEES

19. Rights and duties of allottees.—(*1*) The allottee shall be entitled to obtain the information relating to sanctioned plans, layout plans along with the specifications, approved by the competent authority and such other information as provided in this Act or the rules and regulations made thereunder or the agreement for sale signed with the promoter.

(*2*) The allottee shall be entitled to know stage-wise time schedule of completion of the project, including the provisions for water, sanitation, electricity and other amenities and services as agreed to between the promoter and the allottee in accordance with the terms and conditions of the agreement for sale.

(*3*) The allottee shall be entitled to claim the possession of apartment, plot or building, as the case may be, and the association of allottees shall be entitled to claim the possession of the common areas, as per the declaration given by the promoter under sub-clause (*C*) of clause (*l*) of sub-section (*2*) of section 4.

(*4*) The allottee shall be entitled to claim the refund of amount paid along with interest at such rate as may be prescribed and compensation in the manner as provided under this Act, from the promoter, if the promoter fails to comply or is unable to give possession of the apartment, plot or building, as the case may be, in accordance with the terms of agreement for sale or due to discontinuance of his business as a developer on account of suspension or revocation of his registration under the provisions of this Act or the rules or regulations made thereunder.

(*5*) The allottee shall be entitled to have the necessary documents and plans, including that of common areas, after handing over the physical possession of the apartment or plot or building as the case may be, by the promoter.

(*6*) Every allottee, who has entered into an agreement for sale to take an apartment, plot or building as the case may be, under section 13, shall be responsible to make necessary payments in the manner and within the time as specified in the said agreement for sale and shall pay at the proper time and place, the share of the registration charges, municipal taxes, water and electricity charges, maintenance charges, ground rent, and other charges, if any.

(*7*) The allottee shall be liable to pay interest, at such rate as may be prescribed, for any delay in payment towards any amount or charges to be paid under sub-section (*6*).

(*8*) The obligations of the allottee under sub-section (*6*) and the liability towards interest under sub-section (*7*) may be reduced when mutually agreed to between the promoter and such allottee.

(*9*) Every allottee of the apartment, plot or building as the case may be, shall participate towards the formation of an association or society or cooperative society of the allottees, or a federation of the same.

(*10*) Every allottee shall take physical possession of the apartment, plot or building as the case may be, within a period of two months of the occupancy certificate issued for the said apartment, plot or building, as the case may be.

(*11*) Every allottee shall participate towards registration of the conveyance deed of the apartment, plot or building, as the case may be, as provided under sub-section (*1*) of section 17 of this Act.

CHAPTER V

THE REAL ESTATE REGULATORY AUTHORITY

20. Establishment and incorporation of Real Estate Regulatory Authority.—(*1*) The appropriate Government shall, within a period of one year from the date of coming into force of this Act, by notification, establish an Authority to be known as the Real Estate Regulatory Authority to exercise the powers conferred on it and to perform the functions assigned to it under this Act:

Provided that the appropriate Government of two or more States or Union territories may, if it deems fit, establish one single Authority:

Provided further that the appropriate Government may, if it deems fit, establish more than one Authority in a State or Union territory, as the case may be:

Provided also that until the establishment of a Regulatory Authority under this section, the appropriate Government shall, by order, designate any Regulatory Authority or any officer preferably the Secretary of the department dealing with Housing, as the Regulatory Authority for the purposes under this Act:

Provided also that after the establishment of the Regulatory Authority, all applications, complaints or cases pending with the Regulatory Authority designated, shall stand transferred to the Regulatory Authority so established and shall be heard from the stage such applications, complaints or cases are transferred.

(*2*) The Authority shall be a body corporate by the name aforesaid having perpetual succession and a common seal, with the power, subject to the provisions of this Act, to acquire, hold and dispose of property, both movable and immovable, and to contract, and shall, by the said name, sue or be sued.

21. Composition of Authority.—The Authority shall consist of a Chairperson and not less than two whole time Members to be appointed by the appropriate Government.

22. Qualifications of Chairperson and Members of Authority.—The Chairperson and other Members of the Authority shall be appointed by the appropriate Government on the recommendations of a Selection Committee consisting of the Chief Justice of the High Court or his nominee, the Secretary of the Department dealing with Housing and the Law Secretary, in such manner as may be prescribed, from amongst persons having adequate knowledge of and professional experience of at-least twenty years in case of the Chairperson and fifteen years in the case of the Members in urban development, housing, real estate development, infrastructure, economics, technical experts from relevant fields, planning, law, commerce, accountancy, industry, management, social service, public affairs or administration:

Provided that a person who is, or has been, in the service of the State Government shall not be appointed as a Chairperson unless such person has held the post of Additional Secretary to the Central Government or any equivalent post in the Central Government or State Government:

Provided further that a person who is, or has been, in the service of the State Government shall not be appointed as a member unless such person has held the post of Secretary to the State Government or any equivalent post in the State Government or Central Government.

23. Term of office of Chairperson and Members.—(*1*) The Chairperson and Members shall hold office for a term not exceeding five years from the date on which they enter upon their office, or until they attain the age of sixty-five years, whichever is earlier and shall not be eligible for re-appointment.

(*2*) Before appointing any person as a Chairperson or Member, the appropriate Government shall satisfy itself that the person does not have any such financial or other interest as is likely to affect prejudicially his functions as such Member.

24. Salary and allowances payable to Chairperson and Members.—(*1*) The salary and allowances payable to, and the other terms and conditions of service of, the Chairperson and other Members shall be such as may be prescribed and shall not be varied to their disadvantage during their tenure.

(*2*) Notwithstanding anything contained in sub-sections (*1*) and (*2*) of section 23, the Chairperson or a Member, as the case may be, may,—

    (*a*) relinquish his office by giving in writing, to the appropriate Government, notice of not less than three months; or (*b*) be removed from his office in accordance with the provisions of section 26 of this Act.

(*3*) Any vacancy caused to the office of the Chairperson or any other Member shall be filled-up within a period of three months from the date on which such vacancy occurs.

25. Administrative powers of Chairperson.—The Chairperson shall have powers of general superintendence and directions in the conduct of the affairs of Authority and he shall, in addition to presiding over the meetings of the Authority, exercise and discharge such administrative powers and functions of the Authority as may be prescribed.

26. Removal of Chairperson and Members from office in certain circumstances.—(*1*) The appropriate Government may, in accordance with the procedure notified, remove from office the Chairperson or other Members, if the Chairperson or such other Member, as the case may be,—

(*a*) has been adjudged as an insolvent; or

(*b*) has been convicted of an offence, involving moral turpitude; or

(*c*) has become physically or mentally incapable of acting as a Member; or

(*d*) has acquired such financial or other interest as is likely to affect prejudicially his functions; or

(*e*) has so abused his position as to render his continuance in office prejudicial to the public interest.

(*2*) The Chairperson or Member shall not be removed from his office on the ground specified under clause (*d*) or clause (*e*) of sub-section (*1*) except by an order made by the appropriate Government after an inquiry made by a Judge of the High Court in which such Chairperson or Member has been informed of the charges against him and given a reasonable opportunity of being heard in respect of those charges.

27. Restrictions on Chairperson or Members on employment after cessation of office.—(*1*) The Chairperson or a Member, ceasing to hold office as such, shall not—

(*a*) accept any employment in, or connected with, the management or administration of, any person or organisation which has been associated with any work under this Act, from the date on which he ceases to hold office:

Provided that nothing contained in this clause shall apply to any employment under the appropriate Government or a local authority or in any statutory authority or any corporation established by or under any Central, State or provincial Act or a Government Company, as defined under clause (*45*) of section 2 of the Companies Act, 2013 (18 of 2013), which is not a promoter as per the provisions of this Act;

(*b*) act, for or on behalf of any person or organisation in connection with any specific proceeding or transaction or negotiation or a case to which the Authority is a party and with respect to which the Chairperson or such Member had, before cessation of office, acted for or provided advice to the Authority;

(*c*) give advice to any person using information which was obtained in his capacity as the Chairperson or a Member and being unavailable to or not being able to be made available to the public;

(*d*) enter into a contract of service with, or accept an appointment to a board of directors of, or accept an offer of employment with, an entity with which he had direct and significant official dealings during his term of office as such.

(*2*) The Chairperson and Members shall not communicate or reveal to any person any matter which has been brought under his consideration or known to him while acting as such.

28. Officers and other employees of Authority.—(*1*) The appropriate Government may, in consultation with the Authority appoint such officers and employees as it considers necessary for the efficient discharge of their functions under this Act who would discharge their functions under the general superintendence of the Chairperson.

(*2*) The salary and allowances payable to, and the other terms and conditions of service of, the officers and of the employees of the Authority appointed under sub-section (*1*) shall be such as may be prescribed.

29. Meetings of Authority.—(*1*) The Authority shall meet at such places and times, and shall follow such rules of procedure in regard to the transaction of business at its meetings, (including quorum at such meetings), as may be specified by the regulations made by the Authority.

(*2*) If the Chairperson for any reason, is unable to attend a meeting of the Authority, any other Member chosen by the Members present amongst themselves at the meeting, shall preside at the meeting.

(*3*) All questions which come up before any meeting of the Authority shall be decided by a majority of votes by the Members present and voting, and in the event of an equality of votes, the Chairperson or in his absence, the person presiding shall have a second or casting vote.

(*4*) The questions which come up before the Authority shall be dealt with as expeditiously as possible and the Authority shall dispose of the same within a period of sixty days from the date of receipt of the application:

Provided that where any such application could not be disposed of within the said period of sixty days, the Authority shall record its reasons in writing for not disposing of the application within that period.

30. Vacancies, etc., not to invalidate proceeding of Authority.—No act or proceeding of the Authority shall be invalid merely by reason of—

(*a*) any vacancy in, or any defect in the constitution of, the Authority; or

(*b*) any defect in the appointment of a person acting as a Member of the Authority; or

(*c*) any irregularity in the procedure of the Authority not affecting the merits of the case.

31. Filing of complaints with the Authority or the adjudicating officer.—(*1*) Any aggrieved person may file a complaint with the Authority or the adjudicating officer, as the case may be, for any violation or contravention of the provisions of this Act or the rules and regulations made thereunder, against any promoter, allottee or real estate agent, as the case may be.

Explanation.—For the purpose of this sub-section "person" shall include the association of allottees or any voluntary consumer association registered under any law for the time being in force.

(*2*) The form, manner and fees for filing complaint under sub-section (*1*) shall be such as may be [1][prescribed].

32. Functions of Authority for promotion of real estate sector.—The Authority shall in order to facilitate the growth and promotion of a healthy, transparent, efficient and competitive real estate sector make recommendations to the appropriate Government or the competent authority, as the case may be, on,—

(*a*) protection of interest of the allottees, promoter and real estate agent;

(*b*) creation of a single window system for ensuring time bound project approvals and clearances for timely completion of the project;

(*c*) creation of a transparent and robust grievance redressal mechanism against acts of omission and commission of competent authorities and their officials;

(*d*) measures to encourage investment in the real estate sector including measures to increase financial assistance to affordable housing segment;

(*e*) measures to encourage construction of environmentally sustainable and affordable housing, promoting standardisation and use of appropriate construction materials, fixtures, fittings and construction techniques;

---

1. Subs. by the Real Estate (Regulation and Development) Removal of Difficulties Order, 2016 [S.O. 3347 (E)], for "specified by regulations" (w.e.f. 28-10-2016).

(*f*) measures to encourage grading of projects on various parameters of development including grading of promoters;

(*g*) measures to facilitate amicable conciliation of disputes between the promoters and the allottees through dispute settlement forums set up by the consumer or promoter associations;

(*h*) measures to facilitate digitization of land records and system towards conclusive property titles with title guarantee;

(*i*) to render advice to the appropriate Government in matters relating to the development of real estate sector;

(*j*) any other issue that the Authority may think necessary for the promotion of the real estate sector.

33. Advocacy and awareness measures.—(*1*) The appropriate Government may, while formulating a policy on real estate sector (including review of laws related to real estate sector) or any other matter, make a reference to the Authority for its opinion on possible effect of such policy or law on real estate sector and on the receipt of such a reference, the Authority shall within a period of sixty days of making such reference, give its opinion to the appropriate Government, which may thereafter take further action as it deems fit.

(*2*) The opinion given by the Authority under sub-section (*1*) shall not be binding upon the appropriate Government in formulating such policy or laws.

(*3*) The Authority shall take suitable measures for the promotion of advocacy, creating awareness and imparting training about laws relating to real estate sector and policies.

34. Functions of Authority.—The functions of the Authority shall include—

(*a*) to register and regulate real estate projects and real estate agents registered under this Act;

(*b*) to publish and maintain a website of records, for public viewing, of all real estate projects for which registration has been given, with such details as may be prescribed, including information provided in the application for which registration has been granted;

(*c*) to maintain a database, on its website, for public viewing, and enter the names and photographs of promoters as defaulters including the project details, registration for which has been revoked or have been penalised under this Act, with reasons therefor, for access to the general public;

(*d*) to maintain a database, on its website, for public viewing, and enter the names and photographs of real estate agents who have applied and registered under this Act, with such details as may be prescribed, including those whose registration has been rejected or revoked;

(*e*) to fix through regulations for each areas under its jurisdiction the standard fees to be levied on the allottees or the promoter or the real estate agent, as the case may be;

(*f*) to ensure compliance of the obligations cast upon the promoters, the allottees and the real estate agents under this Act and the rules and regulations made thereunder;

(*g*) to ensure compliance of its regulations or orders or directions made in exercise of its powers under this Act;

(*h*) to perform such other functions as may be entrusted to the Authority by the appropriate Government as may be necessary to carry out the provisions of this Act.

35. Powers of Authority to call for information, conduct investigations.—(*1*) Where the Authority considers it expedient to do so, on a complaint or *suo motu*, relating to this Act or the rules or regulations made thereunder, it may, by order in writing and recording reasons therefor call upon any promoter or allottee or real estate agent, as the case may be, at any time to furnish in writing such information or explanation relating to its affairs as the Authority may require and appoint one or more persons to make an inquiry in relation to the affairs of any promoter or allottee or the real estate agent, as the case may be.

(*2*) Notwithstanding anything contained in any other law for the time being in force, while exercising the powers under sub-section (*1*), the Authority shall have the same powers as are vested in a civil court under the Code of Civil Procedure, 1908 (5 of 1908) while trying a suit, in respect of the following matters, namely:—

(*i*) the discovery and production of books of account and other documents, at such place and at such time as may be specified by the Authority;

(*ii*) summoning and enforcing the attendance of persons and examining them on oath;

(*iii*) issuing commissions for the examination of witnesses or documents;

(*iv*) any other matter which may be prescribed.

36. Power to issue interim orders.—Where during an inquiry, the Authority is satisfied that an act in contravention of this Act, or the rules and regulations made thereunder, has been committed and continues to be committed or that such act is about to be committed, the Authority may, by order, restrain any promoter, allottee or real estate agent from carrying on such act until the conclusion of such inquiry or until further orders, without giving notice to such party, where the Authority deems it necessary.

37. Powers of Authority to issue directions.—The Authority may, for the purpose of discharging its functions under the provisions of this Act or rules or regulations made thereunder, issue such directions from time to time, to the promoters or allottees or real estate agents, as the case may be, as it may consider necessary and such directions shall be binding on all concerned.

38. Powers of Authority.—(*1*) The Authority shall have powers to impose penalty or interest, in regard to any contravention of obligations cast upon the promoters, the allottees and the real estate agents, under this Act or the rules and the regulations made thereunder.

(*2*) The Authority shall be guided by the principles of natural justice and, subject to the other provisions of this Act and the rules made thereunder, the Authority shall have powers to regulate its own procedure.

(*3*) Where an issue is raised relating to agreement, action, omission, practice or procedure that—

(*a*) has an appreciable prevention, restriction or distortion of competition in connection with the development of a real estate project; or

(*b*) has effect of market power of monopoly situation being abused for affecting interest of allottees adversely,

then the Authority, may, *suo motu*, make reference in respect of such issue to the Competition Commission of India.

39. Rectification of orders.—The Authority may, at any time within a period of two years from the date of the order made under this Act, with a view to rectifying any mistake apparent from the record, amend any order passed by it, and shall make such amendment, if the mistake is brought to its notice by the parties:

Provided that no such amendment shall be made in respect of any order against which an appeal has been preferred under this Act:

Provided further that the Authority shall not, while rectifying any mistake apparent from record, amend substantive part of its order passed under the provisions of this Act.

40. Recovery of interest or penalty or compensation and enforcement of order, etc.—(*1*) If a promoter or an allottee or a real estate agent, as the case may be, fails to pay any interest or penalty or compensation imposed on him, by the adjudicating officer or the Regulatory Authority or the Appellate Authority, as the case may be, under this Act or the rules and regulations made thereunder, it shall be recoverable from such promoter or allottee or real estate agent, in such manner as may be prescribed as an arrears of land revenue.

(2) If any adjudicating officer or the Regulatory Authority or the Appellate Tribunal, as the case may be, issues any order or directs any person to do any act, or refrain from doing any act, which it is empowered to do under this Act or the rules or regulations made thereunder, then in case of failure by any person to comply with such order or direction, the same shall be enforced, in such manner as may be prescribed.

CHAPTER VI

CENTRAL ADVISORY COUNCIL

41. Establishment of Central Advisory Council.—(*1*) The Central Government may, by notification, establish with effect from such date as it may specify in such notification, a Council to be known as the Central Advisory Council.

(*2*) The Minister to the Government of India in charge of the Ministry of the Central Government dealing with Housing shall be the *ex officio* Chairperson of the Central Advisory Council.

(*3*) The Central Advisory Council shall consist of representatives of the Ministry of Finance, Ministry of Industry and Commerce, Ministry of Urban Development, Ministry of Consumer Affairs, Ministry of Corporate Affairs, Ministry of Law and Justice, Niti Aayog, National Housing Bank, Housing and Urban Development Corporation, five representatives of State Governments to be selected by rotation, five representatives of the Real Estate Regulatory Authorities to be selected by rotation, and any other Central Government department as notified.

(*4*) The Central Advisory Council shall also consist of not more than ten members to represent the interests of real estate industry, consumers, real estate agents, construction labourers, non-governmental organisations and academic and research bodies in the real estate sector.

42. Functions of Central Advisory Council.—(*1*) The functions of the Central Advisory Council shall be to advise and recommend the Central Government,—

(*a*) on all matters concerning the implementation of this Act;

(*b*) on major questions of policy;

(*c*) towards protection of consumer interest;

(*d*) to foster the growth and development of the real estate sector;

(*e*) on any other matter as may be assigned to it by the Central Government.

(*2*) The Central Government may specify the rules to give effect to the recommendations of the Central Advisory Council on matters as provided under sub-section (*1*).

CHAPTER VII

THE REAL ESTATE APPELLATE TRIBUNAL

43. Establishment of Real Estate Appellate Tribunal.—(*1*) The appropriate Government shall, within a period of one year from the date of coming into force of this Act, by notification, establish an Appellate Tribunal to be known as the — (name of the State/Union territory) Real Estate Appellate Tribunal.

(*2*) The appropriate Government may, if it deems necessary, establish one or more benches of the Appellate Tribunal, for various jurisdictions, in the State or Union territory, as the case may be.

(*3*) Every bench of the Appellate Tribunal shall consist of at least one Judicial Member and one Administrative or Technical Member.

(*4*) The appropriate Government of two or more States or Union territories may, if it deems fit, establish one single Appellate Tribunal:

Provided that, until the establishment of an Appellate Tribunal under this section, the appropriate Government shall designate, by order, any Appellate Tribunal functioning under any law for the time being in force, to be the Appellate Tribunal to hear appeals under the Act:

Provided further that after the Appellate Tribunal under this section is established, all matters pending with the Appellate Tribunal designated to hear appeals, shall stand transferred to the Appellate Tribunal so established and shall be heard from the stage such appeal is transferred.

(5) Any person aggrieved by any direction or decision or order made by the Authority or by an adjudicating officer under this Act may prefer an appeal before the Appellate Tribunal having jurisdiction over the matter:

Provided that where a promoter files an appeal with the Appellate Tribunal, it shall not be entertained, without the promoter first having deposited with the Appellate Tribunal atleast thirty per cent. of the penalty, or such higher percentage as may be determined by the Appellate Tribunal, or the total amount to be paid to the allottee including interest and compensation imposed on him, if any, or with both, as the case may be, before the said appeal is heard.

Explanation.—For the purpose of this sub-section "person" shall include the association of allottees or any voluntary consumer association registered under any law for the time being in force.

44. Application for settlement of disputes and appeals to Appellate Tribunal.—(*1*) The appropriate Government or the competent authority or any person aggrieved by any direction or order or decision of the Authority or the adjudicating officer may prefer an appeal to the Appellate Tribunal.

(*2*) Every appeal made under sub-section (*1*) shall be preferred within a period of sixty days from the date on which a copy of the direction or order or decision made by the Authority or the adjudicating officer is received by the appropriate Government or the competent authority or the aggrieved person and it shall be in such form and accompanied by such fee, as may be prescribed:

Provided that the Appellate Tribunal may entertain any appeal after the expiry of sixty days if it is satisfied that there was sufficient cause for not filling it within that period.

(*3*) On receipt of an appeal under sub-section (*1*), the Appellate Tribunal may after giving the parties an opportunity of being heard, pass such orders, including interim orders, as it thinks fit.

(*4*) The Appellate Tribunal shall send a copy of every order made by it to the parties and to the Authority or the adjudicating officer, as the case may be.

(*5*) The appeal preferred under sub-section (*1*), shall be dealt with by it as expeditiously as possible and endeavour shall be made by it to dispose of the appeal within a period of sixty days from the date of receipt of appeal:

Provided that where any such appeal could not be disposed of within the said period of sixty days, the Appellate Tribunal shall record its reasons in writing for not disposing of the appeal within that period.

(*6*) The Appellate Tribunal may, for the purpose of examining the legality or propriety or correctness of any order or decision of the Authority or the adjudicating officer, on its own motion or otherwise, call for the records relevant to deposing of such appeal and make such orders as it thinks fit.

45. Composition of Appellate Tribunal.—The Appellate Tribunal shall consist of a Chairperson and not less than two whole time Members of which one shall be a Judicial member and other shall be a Technical or Administrative Member, to be appointed by the appropriate Government.

Explanation.—For the purposes of this Chapter,—

(*i*) "Judicial Member" means a Member of the Appellate Tribunal appointed as such under clause (*b*) of sub-section (*1*) of section 46;

(*ii*) "Technical or Administrative Member" means a Member of the Appellate Tribunal appointed as such under clause (*c*) of sub-section (*1*) of section 46.

46. Qualifications for appointment of Chairperson and Members.—(*1*) A person shall not be qualified for appointment as the Chairperson or a Member of the Appellate Tribunal unless he,—

(*a*) in the case of Chairperson, is or has been a Judge of a High Court; and (*b*) in the case of a Judicial Member he has held a judicial office in the territory of India for at least fifteen years or has been a member of the Indian Legal Service and has held the post of Additional Secretary of that service or any equivalent post, or has been an advocate for at least twenty years with experience in dealing with real estate matters; and

(*c*) in the case of a Technical or Administrative Member, he is a person who is well-versed in the field of urban development, housing, real estate development, infrastructure, economics, planning, law, commerce, accountancy, industry, management, public affairs or administration and possesses experience of at least twenty years in the field or who has held the post in the Central Government or a State Government equivalent to the post of Additional Secretary to the Government of India or an equivalent post in the Central Government or an equivalent post in the State Government.

(*2*) The Chairperson of the Appellate Tribunal shall be appointed by the appropriate Government in consultation with the Chief Justice of High Court or his nominee.

(*3*) The Judicial Members and Technical or Administrative Members of the Appellate Tribunal shall be appointed by the appropriate Government on the recommendations of a Selection Committee consisting of the Chief Justice of the High Court or his nominee, the Secretary of the Department handling Housing and the Law Secretary and in such manner as may be prescribed.

47. Term of office of Chairperson and Members.—(*1*) The Chairperson of the Appellate Tribunal or a Member of the Appellate Tribunal shall hold office, as such for a term not exceeding five years from the date on which he enters upon his office, but shall not be eligible for re-appointment:

Provided that in case a person, who is or has been a Judge of a High Court, has been appointed as Chairperson of the Tribunal, he shall not hold office after he has attained the age of sixty-seven years:

Provided further that no Judicial Member or Technical or Administrative Member shall hold office after he has attained the age of sixty-five years.

(*2*) Before appointing any person as Chairperson or Member, the appropriate Government shall satisfy itself that the person does not have any such financial or other interest, as is likely to affect prejudicially his functions as such member.

48. Salary and allowances payable to Chairperson and Members.—(*1*) The salary and allowances payable to, and the other terms and conditions of service of, the Chairperson and other Members shall be such as may be prescribed and shall not be varied to their disadvantage during their tenure.

(*2*) Notwithstanding anything contained in sub-sections (*1*) and (*2*) of section 47, the Chairperson or a Member, as the case may be, may:—

(*a*) relinquish his office by giving in writing to the appropriate Government a notice of not less than three months;

(*b*) be removed from his office in accordance with the provisions of section 49.

(*3*) A vacancy caused to the office of the Chairperson or any other Member, as the case may be, shall be filled-up within a period of three months from the date on which such vacancy occurs.

49. Removal of Chairperson and Member from office in certain circumstances.—(*1*) The appropriate Government may, in consultation with the Chief Justice of the High Court, remove from office of the Chairperson or any Judicial Member or Technical or Administrative Member of the Appellate Tribunal, who—

(*a*) has been adjudged as an insolvent; or

(*b*) has been convicted of an offence which, in the opinion of the appropriate Government involves moral turpitude; or

(*c*) has become physically or mentally incapable; or

(*d*) has acquired such financial or other interest as is likely to affect prejudicially his functions; or (*e*) has so abused his position as to render his continuance in office prejudicial to the public interest.

(*2*) The Chairperson or Judicial Member or Technical or Administrative Member shall not be removed from his office except by an order made by the appropriate Government after an inquiry made by the Judge of the High Court in which such Chairperson or Judicial Member or Technical or Administrative Member has been informed of the charges against him and given a reasonable opportunity of being heard in respect of those charges.

(*3*) The appropriate Government may suspend from the office of the Chairperson or Judicial Member or Technical or Administrative Member in respect of whom a reference of conducting an inquiry has been made to the Judge of the High Court under sub-section (*2*), until the appropriate Government passes an order on receipt of the report of inquiry made by the Judge of the High Court on such reference.

(*4*) The appropriate Government may, by rules, regulate the procedure for inquiry referred to in sub-section (*2*).

50. Restrictions on Chairperson or Judicial Member or Technical or Administrative Member on employment after cessation of office.—(*1*) The Chairperson or Judicial Member or Technical or Administrative Member, ceasing to hold office as such shall not:—

(*a*) accept any employment in, or connected with, the management or administration of, any person or organisation which has been associated with any work under this Act, from the date on which he ceases to hold office:

Provided that nothing contained in this clause shall apply to any employment under the appropriate Government or a local authority or in any statutory authority or any corporation established by or under any Central, State or Provincial Act or a Government Company as defined under clause (*45*) of section 2 of the Companies Act, 2013 (18 of 2013), which is not a promoter as per the provisions of this Act;

(*b*) act, for or on behalf of any person or organisation in connection with any specific proceeding or transaction or negotiation or a case to which the Authority is a party and with respect to which the Chairperson or Judicial Member or Technical or Administrative Member had, before cessation of office, acted for or provided advice to, the Authority;

(*c*) give advice to any person using information which was obtained in his capacity as the Chairperson or Judicial Member or Technical or Administrative Member and being unavailable to or not being able to be made available to the public;

(*d*) enter into a contract of service with, or accept an appointment to a board of directors of, or accept an offer of employment with, an entity with which he had direct and significant official dealings during his term of office as such.

(*2*) The Chairperson or Judicial Member or Technical or Administrative Member shall not communicate or reveal to any person any matter which has been brought under his consideration or known to him while acting as such.

51. Officers and other employees of Appellate Tribunal.—(*1*) The appropriate Government shall provide the Appellate Tribunal with such officers and employees as it may deem fit.

(*2*) The officers and employees of the Appellate Tribunal shall discharge their functions under the general superintendence of its Chairperson.

(*3*) The salary and allowances payable to, and the other terms and conditions of service of, the officers and employees of the Appellate Tribunal shall be such as may be prescribed.

52. Vacancies.—If, for reason other than temporary absence, any vacancy occurs in the office of the Chairperson or a Member of the Appellate Tribunal, the appropriate Government shall appoint another person in accordance with the provisions of this Act to fill the vacancy and the proceedings may be continued before the Appellate Tribunal from the stage at which the vacancy is filled.

53. Powers of Tribunal.—(*1*) The Appellate Tribunal shall not be bound by the procedure laid down by the Code of Civil Procedure, 1908 (5 of 1908) but shall be guided by the principles of natural justice.

(*2*) Subject to the provisions of this Act, the Appellate Tribunal shall have power to regulate its own procedure.

(*3*) The Appellate Tribunal shall also not be bound by the rules of evidence contained in the Indian Evidence Act, 1872 (1 of 1872).

(*4*) The Appellate Tribunal shall have, for the purpose of discharging its functions under this Act, the same powers as are vested in a civil court under the Code of Civil Procedure, 1908 (5 of 1908) in respect of the following matters, namely:—

(*a*) summoning and enforcing the attendance of any person and examining him on oath;

(*b*) requiring the discovery and production of documents;

(*c*) receiving evidence on affidavits;

(*d*) issuing commissions for the examinations of witnesses or documents;

(*e*) reviewing its decisions;

(*f*) dismissing an application for default or directing it *ex parte*; and

(*g*) any other matter which may be prescribed.

(*5*) All proceedings before the Appellate Tribunal shall be deemed to be judicial proceedings within the meaning of sections 193, 219 and 228 for the purposes of section 196 of the Indian Penal Code (45 of 1860), and the Appellate Tribunal shall be deemed to be civil court for the purposes of section 195 and Chapter XXVI of the Code of Criminal Procedure, 1973 (2 of 1974).

54. Administrative powers of Chairperson of Appellate Tribunal.—The Chairperson shall have powers of general superintendence and direction in the conduct of the affairs of Appellate Tribunal and he shall, in addition to presiding over the meetings of the Appellate Tribunal, exercise and discharge such administrative powers and functions of the Appellate Tribunal as may be prescribed.

55. Vacancies, etc., not to invalidate proceeding of Appellate Tribunal.—No act or proceeding of the Appellate Tribunal shall be invalid merely by reason of—

(*a*) any vacancy in, or any defect in the constitution of, the Appellate Tribunal; or

(*b*) any defect in the appointment of a person acting as a Member of the Appellate Tribunal; or

(*c*) any irregularity in the procedure of the Appellate Tribunal not affecting the merits of the case.

56. Right to legal representation.—The applicant or appellant may either appear in person or authorise one or more chartered accountants or company secretaries or cost accountants or legal practitioners or any of its officers to present his or its case before the Appellate Tribunal or the Regulatory Authority or the adjudicating officer, as the case may be.

Explanation.—For the purposes of this section,—

(*a*) "chartered accountant" means a chartered accountant as defined in clause (*b*) of sub-section (*1*) of section 2 of the Chartered Accountants Act, 1949 (38 of 1949) or any other law for the time being in force and who has obtained a certificate of practice under sub-section (*1*) of section 6 of that Act;

(*b*) "company secretary" means a company secretary as defined in clause (*c*) of sub-section (*1*) of section 2 of the Company Secretaries Act, 1980 (56 of 1980) or any other law for the time being in force and who has obtained a certificate of practice under sub-section (*1*) of section 6 of that Act;

(*c*) "cost accountant" means a cost accountant as defined in clause (*b*) of sub-section (*1*) of section 2 of the Cost and Works Accountants Act, 1959 (23 of 1959) or any other law for the time being in force and who has obtained a certificate of practice under sub-section (*1*) of section 6 of that Act;

(*d*) "legal practitioner" means an advocate, vakil or an attorney of any High Court, and includes a pleader in practice.

57. Orders passed by Appellate Tribunal to be executable as a decree.—(*1*) Every order made by the Appellate Tribunal under this Act shall be executable by the Appellate Tribunal as a decree of civil court, and for this purpose, the Appellate Tribunal shall have all the powers of a civil court.

(*2*) Notwithstanding anything contained in sub-section (*1*), the Appellate Tribunal may transmit any order made by it to a civil court having local jurisdiction and such civil court shall execute the order as if it were a decree made by the court.

58. Appeal to High Court.—(*1*) Any person aggrieved by any decision or order of the Appellate Tribunal, may, file an appeal to the High Court, within a period of sixty days from the date of communication of the decision or order of the Appellate Tribunal, to him, on any one or more of the grounds specified in section 100 of the Code of Civil Procedure, 1908 (5 of 1908):

Provided that the High Court may entertain the appeal after the expiry of the said period of sixty days, if it is satisfied that the appellant was prevented by sufficient cause from preferring the appeal in time.

Explanation.—The expression "High Court" means the High Court of a State or Union territory where the real estate project is situated.

(*2*) No appeal shall lie against any decision or order made by the Appellate Tribunal with the consent of the parties.

CHAPTER VIII

Offences, Penalties and Adjudication

59. Punishment for nonregistration under section 3.—(*1*) If any promoter contravenes the provisions of section 3, he shall be liable to a penalty which may extend up to ten per cent. of the estimated cost of the real estate project as determined by the Authority.

(*2*) If any promoter does not comply with the orders, decisions or directions issued under sub-section (*1*) or continues to violate the provisions of section 3, he shall be punishable with imprisonment for a term which may extend up to three years or with fine which may extend up to a further ten per cent. of the estimated cost of the real estate project, or with both.

60. Penalty for contravention of section 4.—If any promoter provides false information or contravenes the provisions of section 4, he shall be liable to a penalty which may extend up to five per cent. of the estimated cost of the real estate project, as determined by the Authority.

61. Penalty for contravention of other provisions of this Act.—If any promoter contravenes any other provisions of this Act, other than that provided under section 3 or section 4, or the rules or regulations made thereunder, he shall be liable to a penalty which may extend up to five per cent. of the estimated cost of the real estate project as determined by the Authority.

62. Penalty for nonregistration and contravention under sections 9 and 10.—If any real estate agent fails to comply with or contravenes the provisions of section 9 or section 10, he shall be liable to a penalty of ten thousand rupees for every day during which such default continues, which may cumulatively extend up to five per cent. of the cost of plot, apartment or building, as the case may be, of the real estate project, for which the sale or purchase has been facilitated as determined by the Authority.

63. Penalty for failure to comply with orders of Authority by promoter.—If any promoter, who fails to comply with, or contravenes any of the orders or directions of the Authority, he shall be liable to a penalty for every day during which such default continues, which may cumulatively extend up to five per cent., of the estimated cost of the real estate project as determined by the Authority.

64. Penalty for failure to comply with orders of Appellate Tribunal by promoter.—If any promoter, who fails to comply with, or contravenes any of the orders, decisions or directions of the

Appellate Tribunal, he shall be punishable with imprisonment for a term which may extend up to three years or with fine for every day during which such default continues, which may cumulatively extend up to ten per cent. of the estimated cost of the real estate project, or with both.

65. Penalty for failure to comply with orders of Authority by real estate agent.—If any real estate agent, who fails to comply with, or contravenes any of the orders or directions of the Authority, he shall be liable to a penalty for every day during which such default continues, which may cumulatively extend up to five per cent., of the estimated cost of plot, apartment or building, as the case may be, of the real estate project, for which the sale or purchase has been facilitated and as determined by the Authority.

66. Penalty for failure to comply with orders of Appellate Tribunal by real estate agent.—If any real estate agent, who fails to comply with, or contravenes any of the orders, decisions or directions of the Appellate Tribunal, he shall be punishable with imprisonment for a term which may extend up to one year or with fine for every day during which such default continues, which may cumulatively extend up to ten per cent. of the estimated cost of plot, apartment or building, as the case may be, of the real estate project, for which the sale or purchase has been facilitated, or with both.

67. Penalty for failure to comply with orders of Authority by allottee.—If any allottee, who fails to comply with, or contravenes any of the orders, decisions or directions of the Authority he shall be liable to a penalty for the period during which such default continues, which may cumulatively extend up to five per cent. of the plot, apartment or building cost, as the case may be, as determined by the Authority.

68. Penalty for failure to comply with orders of Appellate Tribunal by allottee.—If any allottee, who fails to comply with, or contravenes any of the orders or directions of the Appellate Tribunal, as the case may be, he shall be punishable with imprisonment for a term which may extend up to one year or with fine for every day during which such default continues, which may cumulatively extend up to ten per cent. of the plot, apartment or building cost, as the case may be, or with both.

69. Offences by companies.—(*1*) Where an Offence under this Act has been committed by a company, every person who, at the time, the offence was committed was in charge of, or was responsible to the company for the conduct of, the business of the company, as well as the company, shall be deemed to be guilty of the offence and shall be liable to be proceeded against and punished accordingly:

Provided that nothing contained in this sub-section, shall render any such person liable to any punishment under this Act if he proves that the offence was committed without his knowledge or that he had exercised all due diligence to prevent the commission of such offence.

(*2*) Notwithstanding anything contained in sub-section (*1*), where an offence under this Act has been committed by a company, and it is proved that the offence has been committed with the consent or connivance of, or is attributable to, any neglect on the part of any director, manager, secretary or other officer of the company, such director, manager, secretary or other officer shall also be deemed to be guilty of that offence and shall be liable to be proceeded against and punished accordingly.

Explanation.—For the purpose of this section,—

(*a*) "company" means any body corporate and includes a firm, or other association of individuals; and

(*b*) "director" in relation to a firm, means a partner in the firm.

70. Compounding of offences.—Notwithstanding anything contained in the Code of Criminal Procedure, 1973 (2 of 1974), if any person is punished with imprisonment under this Act, the punishment may, either before or after the institution of the prosecution, be compounded by the court on such terms and conditions and on payment of such sums as may be prescribed:

Provided that the sum prescribed shall not, in any case, exceed the maximum amount of the fine which may be imposed for the offence so compounded.

71. Power to adjudicate.—(*1*) For the purpose of adjudging compensation under sections 12, 14, 18 and section 19, the Authority shall appoint, in consultation with the appropriate Government, one or more judicial officer as deemed necessary, who is or has been a District Judge to be an adjudicating officer for holding an inquiry in the prescribed manner, after giving any person concerned a reasonable opportunity of being heard:

Provided that any person whose complaint in respect of matters covered under sections 12, 14, 18 and section 19 is pending before the Consumer Disputes Redressal Forum or the Consumer Disputes Redressal Commission or the National Consumer Redressal Commission, established under section 9 of the Consumer Protection Act, 1986 (68 of 1986), on or before the commencement of this Act, he may, with the permission of such Forum or Commission, as the case may be, withdraw the complaint pending before it and file an application before the adjudicating officer under this Act.

(2) The application for adjudging compensation under sub-section (1), shall be dealt with by the adjudicating officer as expeditiously as possible and dispose of the same within a period of sixty days from the date of receipt of the application:

Provided that where any such application could not be disposed of within the said period of sixty days, the adjudicating officer shall record his reasons in writing for not disposing of the application within that period.

(3) While holding an inquiry the adjudicating officer shall have power to summon and enforce the attendance of any person acquainted with the facts and circumstances of the case to give evidence or to produce any document which in the opinion of the adjudicating officer, may be useful for or relevant to the subject matter of the inquiry and if, on such inquiry, he is satisfied that the person has failed to comply with the provisions of any of the sections specified in sub-section (1), he may direct to pay such compensation or interest, as the case any be, as he thinks fit in accordance with the provisions of any of those sections.

72. Factors to be taken into account by the adjudicating officer.—While adjudging the quantum of compensation or interest, as the case may be, under section 71, the adjudicating officer shall have due regard to the following factors, namely:—

(a) the amount of disproportionate gain or unfair advantage, wherever quantifiable, made as a result of the default;

(b) the amount of loss caused as a result of the default;

(c) the repetitive nature of the default;

(d) such other factors which the adjudicating officer considers necessary to the case in furtherance of justice.

CHAPTER IX

Finance, Accounts, Audits and Reports

73. Grants and loans by Central Government.—The Central Government may, after due appropriation made by Parliament in this behalf, make to the Authority grants and loans of such sums of money as that Government may consider necessary.

74. Grants and loans by State Government.—The State Government may, after due appropriation made by State Legislature by law in this behalf, make to the Authority, grants and loans of such sums of money as the State Government may think fit for being utilised for the purposes of this Act.

75. Constitution of Fund.—(1) The appropriate Government shall constitute a fund to be called the 'Real Estate Regulatory Fund' and there shall be credited thereto,—

(a) all Government grants received by the Authority;

(b) the fees received under this Act;

(c) the interest accrued on the amounts referred to in clauses (a) to (b).

(2) The Fund shall be applied for meeting—

(a) the salaries and allowances payable to the Chairperson and other Members, the adjudicating officer and the administrative expenses including the salaries and allowances payable to the officers and other employees of the Authority and the Appellate Tribunal;

(b) the other expenses of the Authority in connection with the discharge of its functions and for the purposes of this Act.

(3) The Fund shall be administered by a committee of such Members of the Authority as may be determined by the Chairperson.

(4) The committee appointed under sub-section (3) shall spend monies out of the Fund for carrying out the objects for which the Fund has been constituted.

76. Crediting sums realised by way of penalties to Consolidated Fund of India or State account.—(1) All sums realised, by way of penalties, imposed by the Appellate Tribunal or the Authority, in the Union territories, shall be credited to the Consolidated Fund of India.

(2) All sums realised, by way of penalties, imposed by the Appellate Tribunal or the Authority, in a State, shall be credited to such account as the State Government may specify.

77. Budget, accounts and audit.—(1) The Authority shall prepare a budget, maintain proper accounts and other relevant records and prepare an annual statement of accounts in such form as may be prescribed by the appropriate Government in consultation with the Comptroller and Auditor General of India.

(2) The accounts of the Authority shall be audited by the Comptroller and Auditor General of India at such intervals as may be specified by him and any expenditure incurred in connection with such audit shall be payable by the Authority to the Comptroller and Auditor General of India.

(3) The Comptroller and Auditor-General and any person appointed by him in connection with the audit of the accounts of the Authority under this Act shall have the same rights and privileges and authority in connection with such audit as the Comptroller and Auditor General generally has in connection with the audit of Government accounts and, in particular shall have the right to demand and production of books, accounts, connected vouchers and other documents and papers, and to inspect any of the offices of the Authority.

(4) The accounts of the Authority, as certified by the Comptroller and Auditor-General of India or any other person appointed by him in this behalf, together with the audit report thereon shall be forwarded annually to the appropriate Government by the Authority and the appropriate Government shall cause the audit report to be laid, as soon as may be after it is received, before each House of Parliament or, as the case may be, before the State Legislature or the Union territory Legislature, where it consists of two Houses, or where such legislature consists of one House, before that House.

78. Annual report.—(1) The Authority shall prepare once in every year, in such form and at such time as may be prescribed by the appropriate Government,—

(a) a description of all the activities of the Authority for the previous year;

(b) the annual accounts for the previous year; and

(c) the programmes of work for the coming year.

(2) A copy of the report received under sub-section (1) shall be laid, as soon as may be after it is received, before each House of Parliament or, as the case may be, before the State Legislature or the Union Territory Legislature, where it consists of two Houses, or where such legislature consists of one House, before that House.

CHAPTER X

MISCELLANEOUS

79. Bar of jurisdiction.—No civil court shall have jurisdiction to entertain any suit or proceeding in respect of any matter which the Authority or the adjudicating officer or the Appellate Tribunal is empowered by or under this Act to determine and no injunction shall be granted by any court or other authority in respect of any action taken or to be taken in pursuance of any power conferred by or under this Act.

80. Cognizance of offences.—(*1*) No court shall take cognizance of any offence punishable under this Act or the rules or regulations made thereunder save on a complaint in writing made by the Authority or by any officer of the Authority duly authorised by it for this purpose.

(*2*) No court inferior to that of a Metropolitan Magistrate or a Judicial Magistrate of the first class shall try any offence punishable under this Act.

81. Delegation.—The Authority may, by general or special order in writing, delegate to any member, officer of the Authority or any other person subject to such conditions, if any, as may be specified in the order, such of its powers and functions under this Act (except the power to make regulations under section 85), as it may deem necessary.

82. Power of appropriate Government to supersede Authority.—(*1*) If, at any time, the appropriate Government is of the opinion,—

(*a*) that, on account of circumstances beyond the control of the Authority, it is unable to discharge the functions or perform the duties imposed on it by or under the provisions of this Act; or

(*b*) that the Authority has persistently defaulted in complying with any direction given by the appropriate Government under this Act or in the discharge of the functions or performance of the duties imposed on it by or under the provisions of this Act and as a result of such default the financial position of the Authority or the administration of the Authority has suffered; or

(*c*) that circumstances exist which render it necessary in the public interest so to do,

the appropriate Government may, by notification, supersede the Authority for such period, not exceeding six months, as may be specified in the notification and appoint a person or persons as the President or the Governor, as the case may be, may direct to exercise powers and discharge functions under this Act:

Provided that before issuing any such notification, the appropriate Government shall give a reasonable opportunity to the Authority to make representations against the proposed supersession and shall consider the representations, if any, of the Authority.

(*2*) Upon the publication of a notification under sub-section (*1*) superseding the Authority,—

(*a*) the Chairperson and other Members shall, as from the date of supersession, vacate their offices as such;

(*b*) all the powers, functions and duties which may, by or under the provisions of this Act, be exercised or discharged by or on behalf of the Authority shall, until the Authority is reconstituted under sub-section (*3*), be exercised and discharged by the person or persons referred to in sub-section (*1*); and

(*c*) all properties owned or controlled by the Authority shall, until the Authority is reconstituted under sub-section (*3*), vest in the appropriate Government.

(*3*) On or before the expiration of the period of supersession specified in the notification issued under sub-section (*1*), the appropriate Government shall reconstitute the Authority by a fresh appointment of its Chairperson and other members and in such case any person who had vacated his office under clause (*a*) of sub-section (*2*) shall not be deemed to be disqualified for re-appointment.

(*4*) The appropriate Government shall cause a copy of the notification issued under sub-section (*1*) and a full report of any action taken under this section and the circumstances leading to such action to be laid before each House of Parliament or, as the case may be, before the State Legislature, or the Union

Territory Legislature, as the case may be, where it consists of two Houses, or where such legislature consists of one House, before that House.

83. Powers of appropriate Government to issue directions to Authority and obtain reports and returns.—(*1*) Without prejudice to the foregoing provisions of this Act, the Authority shall, in exercise of its powers and in performance of its functions under this Act, be bound by such directions on questions of policy, as the appropriate Government may give in writing to it from time to time:

Provided that the Authority shall, as far as practicable, be given an opportunity to express its views before any direction is given under this sub-section.

(*2*) If any dispute arises between the appropriate Government and the Authority as to whether a question is or is not a question of policy, the decision of the appropriate Government thereon shall be final.

(*3*) The Authority shall furnish to the appropriate Government such returns or other information with respect to its activities as the appropriate Government may, from time to time, require.

84. Power of appropriate Government to make rules.—(*1*) The appropriate Government shall, within a period of six months of the commencement of this Act, by notification, make rules for carrying out the provisions of this Act.

(*2*) In particular, and without prejudice to the generality of the foregoing power, such rules may provide for all or any of the following matters, namely:—

[1][(*a*) the form, time and manner of making application and fees payable therewith under sub-section (*1*) of section 4;

(*ab*) information and documents for application to the Authority for registration under clause (*m*) of sub-section (*2*) of section 4;

(*ac*) the form of application and the fees for extension of registration under section 6;]

(*b*) the form and manner of making application and fee and documents to be accompanied with such application as under sub-section (*2*) of section 9;

(*c*) the period, manner and conditions under which the registration is to be granted under sub-section (*3*) of section 9;

(*d*) the validity of the period of registration and the manner and fee for renewal under sub-section (*6*) of section 9;

(*e*) the maintenance and preservation of books of account, records and documents under clause (*b*) of section 10;

(*f*) the discharge of other functions by the real estate agent under clause (*e*) of section 10;

(*g*) the rate of interest payable under section 12;

(*h*) the form and particulars of agreement for sale under sub-section (*2*) of section 13;

(*i*) the rate of interest payable under clause (*b*) of sub-section (*1*) of section 18;

(*j*) the rate of interest payable under sub-section (*4*) of section 19;

(*k*) the rate of interest payable under sub-section (*7*) of section 19;

(*l*) the manner of selection of Chairperson and Members of Authority under section 22;

(*m*) the salaries and allowances payable to, and the other terms and conditions of service of, the Chairperson and other Members of the Authority under sub-section (*1*) of section 24;

(*n*) the administrative powers of the Chairpersons under section 25;

---

1. Subs. by the Real Estate (Regulation and Development) Removal of Difficulties Order, 2016 [S.O. 3347(E)], for clause (*a*) (w.e.f. 28-10-2016).

(*o*) the salaries and allowances payable to, and the other terms and conditions of service of, the officers and other employees of the Authority under sub-section (*2*) of section 28;

¹[(*oa*) the form, manner and fees for filing of a complaint under sub-section (*2*) of section 31;]

(*p*) the details to be published on the website as under clause (*b*) and under clause (*d*) of section 34;

(*q*) the additional functions which may be performed by the Authority under clause (*iv*) of sub-section (*2*) of section 35;

(*r*) the manner of recovery of interest, penalty and compensation under sub-section (*1*) of section 40;

(*s*) the manner of implementation of the order, direction or decisions of the adjudicating officer, the Authority or the Appellate Tribunal under sub-section (*2*) of section 40;

(*t*) recommendations received from the Central Advisory Council under sub-section (*2*) of section 42;

(*u*) the form and manner and fee for filing of appeal under sub-section (*2*) of section 44;

(*v*) the manner of selection of Members of the Tribunal under sub-section (*3*) of section 46;

(*w*) the salaries and allowances payable to, and the other terms and conditions of service of, the Chairperson and other Members of the Appellate Tribunal under sub-section (*1*) of section 48;

(*x*) the procedure for inquiry of the charges against the Chairperson or Judicial Member of the Tribunal under sub-section (*4*) of section 49;

(*y*) the salaries and allowances payable to, and the other terms and conditions of service of, the officers and employees of the Appellate Tribunal under sub-section (*3*) of section 51;

(*z*) any other powers of the Tribunal under clause (*g*) of sub-section (*4*) of section 53;

(*za*) the powers of the Chairperson of the Appellate Tribunal under section 54;

(*zb*) the terms and conditions and the payment of such sum for compounding of the offences under section 70;

(*zc*) the manner of inquiry under sub-section (*1*) of section 71;

(*zd*) the form to be specified in which the Authority shall prepare a budget, maintain proper accounts and other relevant records and prepare an annual statement of accounts under sub-section (*1*) of section 77;

(*ze*) the form in which and time at which the Authority shall prepare an annual report under sub-section (*1*) of section 78;

(*zf*) any other matter which is to be, or may be, prescribed, or in respect of which provision is to be made, by rules.

85. Power to make regulations.—(*1*) The Authority shall, within a period of three months of its establishment, by notification, make regulations, consistent with this Act and the rules made thereunder to carry out the purposes of this Act.

(*2*) In particular, and without prejudice to the generality of the foregoing power, such regulations may provide for all or any of the following matters, namely:—

²*   *   *   *   *

(*c*) such other information and documents required under clause (*f*) of sub-section (*1*) of section 11;

---

1. Ins. by the Real Estate (Regulation and Development) Removal of Difficulties Order, 2016 [S.O. 3347(E)], (w.e.f. 28-10-2016).
2. Omitted by *ibid*. (w.e.f. 28-10-2016).

(*d*) display of sanctioned plans, layout plans along with specifications, approved by the competent authority, for display under clause (*a*) of sub-section (*3*) of section 11;

(*e*) preparation and maintenance of other details under sub-section (*6*) of section 11;

(*f*) time, places and the procedure in regard to transaction of business at the meetings of the Authority under sub-section (*1*) of section 29;

[1]*   *   *   *   *

(*h*) standard fees to be levied on the promoter, the allottees or the real estate agent under clause (*e*) of section 34;

(*i*) any other matter which is required to be, or may be, specified by regulation or in respect of which provision is to be made by regulations.

86. Laying of rules. —(*1*) Every rule made by the Central Government, every regulation made by the Authority under the Union territory of Delhi and the Union territories without Legislature and every notification issued by the Central Government under this Act shall be laid, as soon as may be after it is made, before each House of Parliament, while it is in session, for a total period of thirty days which may be comprised in one session or in two or more successive sessions, and if, before the expiry of the session immediately following the session or the successive sessions aforesaid, both Houses agree in making any modification in the rule or regulation or in the notification, as the case may be, or both Houses agree that the rule or regulation or the notification should not be made, the rule or regulation or notification, as the case may be, shall thereafter have effect only in such modified form or be of no effect, as the case may be; so, however, that any such modification or annulment shall be without prejudice to the validity of anything previously done under that rule or regulation or notification, as the case may be.

(*2*) Every rule made by a State Government or the Union territory Government, as the case may be, every regulation made by the Authority under the State Government or the Union territory Government of Puducherry, as the case may be, and every notification issued by the State Government or the Union territory Government of Puducherry, as the case may be, under this Act, shall be laid as soon as may be, after it is made, before the State Legislature, or the Union territory Legislature, as the case may be, where it consists of two Houses, or where such legislature consists of one House, before that House.

87. Members, etc., to be public servants.—The Chairperson, Members and other officers and employees of the Authority, and the Appellate Tribunal and the adjudicating officer shall be deemed to be public servants within the meaning of section 21 of the Indian Penal Code (45 of 1860).

88. Application of other laws not barred.—The provisions of this Act shall be in addition to, and not in derogation of, the provisions of any other law for the time being in force.

89. Act to have overriding effect.—The provisions of this Act shall have effect, notwithstanding anything inconsistent therewith contained in any other law for the time being in force.

90. Protection of action taken in good faith.—No suit, prosecution or other legal proceedings shall lie against the appropriate Government or the Authority or any officer of the appropriate Government or any member, officer or other employees of the Authority for anything which is in good faith done or intended to be done under this Act or the rules or regulations made thereunder.

91. Power to remove difficulties.—(*1*) If any difficulty arises in giving effect to the provisions of this Act, the Central Government may, by order, published in the Official Gazette, make such provisions not inconsistent with the provisions of this Act as may appear to be necessary for removing the difficulty:

Provided that no order shall be made under this section after the expiry of two years from the date of the commencement of this Act.

(*2*) Every order made under this section shall be laid, as soon as may be after it is made, before each House of Parliament.

92. Repeal. —The Maharashtra Housing (Regulation and Development) Act, 2012 (Maharashtra Act No. II of 2014) is hereby repealed.

---

1. Omitted by the Real Estate (Regulation and Development) Removal of Difficulties Order, 2016 [S.O. 3347 (E)], (w.e.f. 28-10-2016).

NOTIFICATION

Urban Development and Urban Housing Department
Sachivalaya, Gandhinagar
Dated the 4th May, 2017

Real Estate (Regulation and Development) Act, 2016

No. GH/V/82 of 2017/MIS-102017-328145-L:- In exercise of the power conferred by section 84 of the Real Estate (Regulation and Development) Act, 2016 (16 of 2016), the Government of Gujarat hereby makes the following rules, namely:-

CHAPTER I
PRELIMINARY

1. Short title and Commencement

(1) These rules may be called the Gujarat Real Estate (Regulation and Development) (General) Rules, 2017.

(2) It shall come into force with effect from 1st May, 2017.

2. Definitions.- (1) In these rules, unless the context otherwise requires, -

(a) "Act" means the Real Estate (Regulation and Development) Act, 2016;
(b) "Annexure" means an annexure appended to these rules;
(c) "association of allottees" means a collective of the allottees of a real estate project, by whatever name called, registered under any law for the time being in force, acting as group to serve the cause of its members, and shall include the authorised representatives of the allottees;
(d) "authenticated copy" shall mean a self-attested copy of any document required to be provided by any person under these rules;
(e) "Form" means a form appended to these rules;
(f) "appropriate government" means the State Government;
(g) "layout plan" means a plan of the project depicting the division or proposed division of land into plots, roads, open spaces, amenities, etc. and other details as may be necessary;
(h) "project land" means any parcel or parcels of land on which the project is developed and constructed by a promoter; and
(i) "section" means a section of the Act;

(2) Words and expressions used herein and not defined, but defined in the Act, shall have the same meaning respectively assigned to them in the Act.

CHAPTER II
REAL ESTATE PROJECT

3. Information and documents to be furnished by the promoter for registration of project.-

(1) The promoter shall furnish the following additional information and documents, along with those specified under the relevant sections of the Act, for registration of the real estate project with the regulatory authority namely:-
   (a) Authenticated copy of the PAN card of the promoter
   (b) Name, photograph, contact details and address of the promoter if he is an individual or authorised representative; or the name, photograph, contact details and address of the chairman, partners, directors, as the case may be, and the

authorised representative in case of other entities;

(c) The number of open parking areas and the number of covered parking areas available in the said real estate project;

(d) Copy of the legal title deed reflecting the title of the promoter to the land on which development is proposed to be developed along with legally valid documents with authentication of such title, if such land is owned by another person;

(e) The details of encumbrances on the land on which development is proposed including any rights, title, interest or name of any party in or over such land along with details;

(f) Where the promoter is not the owner of the land on which development is proposed details of the consent of the owner of the land along with a copy of the collaboration agreement, development agreement, joint development agreement or any other agreement, as the case may be, entered into between the promoter and such owner and copies of title and other documents reflecting the title of such owner on the land proposed to be developed;

(2) The application referred to in sub-section (1) of section 4 shall be made in writing as per Form 'A', which shall be submitted in triplicate, until the application procedure is made web based as provided under sub-section (3) of section 4 of the Act.

(3) The promoter shall pay a registration fee at the time of application for registration by way of a demand draft drawn on any scheduled bank, for a sum calculated at the rate of:-

(a) In case of group housing project,- five rupees per square meter for projects where the area of land proposed to be developed does not exceed one thousand square meters; or rupees ten per square meter for projects where the area of land proposed to be developed exceeds one thousand square meters, but shall not be more than five lakhs rupees;

(b) In case of mixed development (residential and commercial) project,- ten rupees per square meter for projects where the area of land proposed to be developed does not exceed one thousand square meters; or fifteen rupees per square meter for projects where the area of land proposed to be developed exceeds one thousand square meters, but shall not be more than seven lakhs rupees;

(c) In case of commercial projects,- twenty rupees per square meter for projects where the area of land proposed to be developed does not exceed one thousand square meters; or twenty five rupees per square meter for projects where the area of land proposed to be developed exceeds one thousand square meters, but shall not be more than ten lakhs rupees;

(d) In case of plotted development projects,- five rupees per square meter, but shall not be more than two lakhs rupees.

(4) The declaration to be submitted under clause (l) of sub-section (2) of section 4 of the Act, shall be as per Form 'B'.

(5) In case the promoter applies for withdrawal of application for registration of the project before the expiry of the period of 30 days provided under sub-section (1) of section 5, registration fee to the extent of ten percent paid under sub-rules (3) above, or rupees fifty thousand whichever is more, shall be retained as processing fee by the regulatory authority and the remaining amount shall be refunded to the promoter within thirty days from the date of such withdrawal.

(6) The promoter shall disclose,-
estimated cost of real estate project as envisaged by the promoter by bifurcating the same into the market value of the land/ lease charges (as determined by the Government Approved Valuer), cost of construction, other costs, interest, taxes, cess, development and other charges and all other charges/cost in relation to the project in two stages, i.e. before the application is made to the Authority for registration of the real estate project and subsequent to the grant of the registration; the means of financing the real estate project along with the cost already incurred and paid by the promoter out of the estimated cost of the real estate project duly certified and signed by the chartered accountant;

4. **Disclosure by promoters of ongoing projects.-**
(1) Upon the notification for commencement of sub-section (1) of section 3, the promoter of an ongoing project which has not received completion certificate shall, within the time specified in the said sub-section, make an application to the Authority as provided in rule 3.
(2) The promoter shall in addition to disclosures provided in rule 3 disclose the following information, namely:-
   (a) the original sanctioned plan, layout plan and specifications and the subsequent modifications carried out, if any, including the existing sanctioned plan, layout plan and specifications;
   (b) the total amount of the money collected and the balance money to be collected from the allottees at the time of registration of the existing project;
   (c) status of the project (extent of development carried out till date and the extent of development pending) and the time period within which he undertakes to complete the pending project and this information shall be certified by an engineer, an architect and a chartered accountant in practice.

(3) The promoter shall disclose the size of the apartment based on carpet area even if earlier sold on any other basis such as super area, super built up area, built up area etc. which shall not affect the validity of the agreement entered into between the promoter and the allottee to that extent.

(4) In case of plotted development, the promoter shall disclose the area of the plot being sold to the allottees as per the layout plan.

(5) For projects that are ongoing and have not received completion certificate, on the date of commencement of the Act, the promoter shall, within a period of three months of the application for registration of the project with the Authority, deposit in the separate bank account, seventy per cent. of the balance amounts which are to be realized from the allottees, and shall be withdrawn from the separate account, in the manner permissible under rule 5.

5. **Withdrawal of sums deposited in separate account.-** Pursuant to the amounts deposited in a separate account as mentioned in sub-clause (D) of clause (l) of sub-section (2) of section 4 of the Act, the promoter shall be entitled to withdraw the amounts from the separate account in the following manner:
(1) The promoter, at the outset, shall be entitled to withdraw the amounts from the separate account to the extent of the cost already incurred and paid by the promoter, and as duly reflected in the estimated cost of the real estate project, furnished under sub-rule (6) of rule 3, before the date of the application made to the Authority for the registration of the real estate project. Such withdrawal, from time to time, shall be duly certified by a Chartered Accountant.

(2) The cost of the land as mentioned in the estimated cost of the real estate project, to the extent which is not withdrawn as per sub-rule (1) above, shall be entitled for withdrawal by the promoter, from time to time, to the extent of the cost of the land which is incurred and paid by the promoter after the registration of the real estate project by the Authority. Such withdrawal, from time to time, shall be duly certified by a Chartered Accountant.

(3) The promoter shall be entitled to withdraw the balance amount (other than those mentioned in sub-rule (1) and sub-rule (2)) from the separate account only in proportion to the percentage of completion of the project. Further, upon the issuance of the completion certificate for the project, the promoter shall be entitled to withdraw all the remaining amounts which may be lying in a separate account.

(4) That the balance amount as mentioned in sub-rule (3) above, shall be withdrawn by the promoter from the separate account after it is certified (i) by an engineer that the items shown in the cost of construction is matching to the physical condition at the site of the real estate project; (ii) by an architect that the physical condition at the site is built-up as per the sanctioned plan as approved by the competent authority; and (iii) by a chartered accountant in respect of the cost already incurred for the purpose of calculating the proportionate cost of completion of the project.

6. Grant or rejection of registration of the project.- (1) Upon the registration of any real estate project as per section 5 read with rule 3, the Authority shall issue to the Promoter a Registration Certificate with a project registration number, in Form "C". The period for which registration shall be valid shall exclude such period where actual work could not be carried by the promoter as per sanctioned plan due to specific stay or injunction orders relating to the real estate project from any Court of law, or Tribunal, competent authority, statutory authority, high power committee etc., or due to such mitigating circumstances as may be decided by the Regulatory Authority:

Provided that, while deciding on such mitigating circumstances, the Authority shall give reasonable opportunity of hearing to the allottees and such other person, who in the opinion of the Authority, have interest in the project.

(2) In case of the rejection of the application in accordance with the section 5, the Regulatory Authority, shall inform to the applicant in Form "D" as also to the concerned Competent Authority or Statutory Authorities:

Provided that, no application for registration of any real estate project shall be rejected unless the Promoter has been given adequate opportunity of being heard in the matter by the Authority.

7. Extension of registration of the project.- (1) An application for extension of the real estate project shall be made to the Authority, in Form "E", along with an explanatory note setting out the grounds and reasons for delay in the completion of the real estate project and the need for extension, along with documents supporting such grounds and reasons:

Provided that, where extension of registration is due to *force majeure* the Authority may at its discretion waive the fee for such extension granted to any real estate project.

(2) The grant of extension of registration to a real estate project, shall be in Form "F". The Authority shall supply a copy thereto to the Promoter and in case of rejection of the application for extension of registration, the authority shall, after giving to the applicant an opportunity of being heard as provided in the second proviso of section 6, inform the promoter about the same, in Form "D". The intimation thereof shall also be given to the respective Competent Authority and Statutory Authorities.

(3) The application for extension of Real Estate Project shall be accompanied with fees for an amount equivalent to half the registration fees as prescribed under sub-rule (3) of rule-3.

8. Revocation of Registration of the project.- (1) Upon the revocation of registration of a project as per section 7 the regulatory authority shall inform the promoter about such revocation as per Form 'D'.

(2) The registration granted to the promoter under section 5 shall not be revoked unless the Authority has given to the promoter not less than thirty days' notice, in writing, stating the ground on which it proposes to revoke the registration, and has considered any cause shown by the promoter within the said period:

Provided that, prior to the revocation of registration of real estate project, the Authority shall also give notice to the concerned competent authority which has granted approval to the real estate project and association of allottees (if any). In case the association of allottees is not formed, the Authority may in its discretion, also give notice to the allottees, to submit their say in that behalf. The Authority while facilitating the remaining development works to be carried out in accordance with the provisions of section 8 shall also take such measures as may be required to protect the interest of other parties who through mortgage or other investments are interested in the real estate project, which are disclosed by the promoter on the Website of the Regulatory Authority:

Provided further that, the Regulatory Authority shall also give adequate opportunity of being heard to any party which through defined instrument of debt or equity have created third party interest in the real estate projects.

Explanation. - For the purposes of the second proviso, the party shall include Scheduled Banks, Housing Finance Companies, Insurance Companies, Non-Banking Finance Companies operating as Asset Finance Companies, Investment Companies, Loan Companies, Investment Finance Companies, Infrastructure Debt Funds, Micro-finance Institutions, Foreign Direct Investors, Private Equity Funds and the Real Estate Investment Trust.

9. Agreement for sale.- (1) For the purpose of sub-section (2) of section 13, the agreement for sale shall be in the form as per Annexure 'A', with such variations as the promoter and the Allottee may agree upon. Provided that the said agreement for sale shall not violate the provisions of the Act or the rules and regulations framed thereunder.

(2) Any application letter, allotment letter or any other document signed by the Allottee, in respect of the apartment, plot or building, prior to the execution and registration of the agreement for sale for such apartment, plot or building, as the case may be, shall not be construed to limit the rights and interests of the Allottee under the agreement for sale or under the Act or the rules or the regulations made thereunder.

CHAPTER III
REAL ESTATE AGENT

10. Application for Registration by the real estate agent.- (1) Every real estate agent required to register as per sub-section (2) of section 9 of the Act. shall make an application in writing to the Regulatory Authority in Form 'G', in triplicate, until the application procedure is made web based, along with the following documents, namely:-

(a) Brief details of his enterprise including its name, registered address, type of enterprise (proprietorship, societies, partnership, company etc.);

(b) Particulars of registration (whether as a proprietorship, partnership, company, society etc.) including the bye-laws, memorandum of association, articles of association etc. as the case may be;

(c) Name, address, contact details and photograph of the real estate agent, if it is an individual and the name, address, contact details and photograph of the partners, directors etc. in case of other entities;

(d) Authenticated copy of the PAN card;

(e) Authenticated copy of the address proof of the place of business.

(2) The real estate agent shall pay a registration fee at the time of application for registration by way of a demand draft or a bankers cheque drawn on any scheduled bank or through online payment, as the case may be, for a sum of ten thousand rupees in case of the applicant being an individual or fifty thousand rupees in case of the applicant other than an individual.

11. Grant of Registration to the real estate agent.- (1) Upon the registration of a real estate agent as per section 9 of the Act. read with Rule 10, the Regulatory Authority shall issue a registration certificate with a registration number as per Form 'H' to the real estate agent.

(2) In case of rejection of the application as per section 9 of the Act. the Regulatory Authority shall inform the applicant as per Form 'I'.

(3) The registration granted under this rule shall be valid for a period five years.

12. Renewal of registration of real estate agent.- (1) The registration granted to a real estate agent under the Act, may be renewed, on an application made by the real estate agent in Form 'J', in triplicate, until the application procedure is made web based, which shall not be less than three months prior to the expiry of the registration granted.

(2) The application for renewal of registration shall be accompanied with a demand draft or a bankers cheque drawn on any scheduled bank or through online payment, as the case may be, for a sum of five thousand rupees in case of the real estate agent being an individual or twenty five thousand rupees in case of the real estate agent other than an individual.

(3) The real estate agent shall also submit all the updated documents set out in clauses (a) to (e) of sub-rule (1) of rule 10 at the time of application for renewal.

(4) In case of renewal of registration, the Regulatory Authority shall inform the real estate agent about the same in Form 'K' and in case of rejection of the application for renewal of

registration the Regulatory Authority, shall inform the real estate agent in Form 'I':

Provided that no application for renewal of registration shall be rejected, unless the applicant has been given an opportunity of being heard in the matter:

Provided further that the Regulatory Authority may grant an opportunity to the real estate agent to rectify the defects in the application within such time period as may be specified by it.

(5) The renewal granted under this rule shall be valid for a period of five years.

13. **Revocation of Registration of real estate agent.-** The Regulatory Authority may, due to reasons specified under sub-section (7) of section 9, revoke the registration granted to the real estate agent or renewal thereof, as the case may be, and intimate the real estate agent of such revocation as per Form 'I'.

14. **Maintenance and preservation of books of accounts, records and documents.-** The real estate agent shall maintain and preserve books of account, records and documents in accordance with the provisions of the Income Tax Act, 1961 (43 of 1961), as amended from time to time, and the rules made thereunder.

15. **Other functions of a real estate agent.-** The real estate agent shall provide assistance to enable the allottee and promoter to exercise their respective rights and fulfil their respective obligations at the time of booking and sale of any plot, apartment or building, as the case may be.

CHAPTER IV
RATE OF INTEREST PAYABLE BY PROMOTER AND ALLOTTEE AND TIMELINES FOR REFUND

16. **Rate of interest payable by the promoter and the Allottee.-** (1) For the purpose of payment of interest under sections 12, 18 and 19 of the Act, the rate of interest shall be the contractual rate of interest as may be mutually agreed to between the promoter and the allottee.

Provided that the rate of interest chargeable from the allottee by the promoter, in case of default by the allottee, shall be equal to the rate of interest which the promoter shall be liable to pay the allottee, in case of default by the promoter.

(2) Where no contractual rate of interest is mutually agreed upon between the promoter and the allottee under sub-rule (1), the rate of interest payable by the promoter to the allottee or by the allottee to the promoter, as the case may be, shall be the rate which is prevalent as per existing directives of Reserve Bank of India i.e. Marginal Cost of Lending Rate (MCLR) the State Bank of India Prime Lending Rate plus two percent.

(3) For the purpose of sub-rule (1) and sub-rule (2), the interest payable by the promoter to the allottee shall be from the date the promoter received the amount or any part thereof till the date the amount or part thereof and interest thereon is refunded, and the interest payable by the allottee to the promoter shall be from the date the allottee defaults in payment to the promoter till the date it is paid.

17. **Timelines for refund.-** Any refund of monies along with the applicable interest and compensation, if any, payable by the promoter in terms of the Act or the rules and regulations made thereunder, shall be payable by the promoter to the allottee within forty-five days from

the date on which such refund along with applicable interest and compensation, if any, becomes due.

CHAPTER V
CENTRAL ADVISORY COUNCIL

18. Manner of giving effect to the recommendation of the Central Advisory Council.-

(1) Pursuant to its establishment in accordance with the sub-section (1) of section 41 of the Act the Central Advisory Council shall, at such intervals as it may deem necessary, make recommendation on the matters set out in sub-section (1) of section 42 of the Act.

(2) The Central Advisory Council shall prepare draft recommendation and invite comments on the same from stakeholders, experts, civil society etc.

(3) Upon receipt of comments on the draft recommendation as per sub-rule (2), the Central Advisory Council shall finalize its recommendation after incorporating such comments as it may deem appropriate and refer the same to the Central Government, who shall have the authority-
   (a) to accept such recommendation in entirety;
   (b) to accept such recommendation with such amendments as it may deem fit and proper;
   (c) to refer back such recommendation to the Central Advisory Council with its comments for consideration;
   (d) to reject such recommendation.

(4) Pursuant to acceptance of the recommendations or part thereof the Central Government may share the recommendation of the Central Advisory Council with the appropriate Government of States and Union Territories with Legislature for further necessary action to give effect to the said recommendation.

(5) As regards, the Union territories without Legislature, the Central Government may, if it deems fit, by notification, make rules to give effect to such recommendations of the Central Advisory Council.

CHAPTER VI OFFENCES AND PENALTIES

19. Terms and conditions and the fine payable for compounding of offence.- (1) The court shall, for the purposes of compounding any offence specified under section 70, accept a sum of money as specified in the Table below:

Offence	Money to be paid for compounding the offence
Imprisonment under sub section (2) of section 59	5% of the estimated cost of the real estate project
Imprisonment under section 64	5% of the estimated cost of the real estate project
Imprisonment under section 66	5% of the estimated cost of the plot, apartment or building, as the case may be, of the real estate project, for which the sale or purchase has been facilitated
Imprisonment under section 68	5% of the estimated cost of the plot, apartment or building, as the case may be

Provided that the State Government may, by notification in the official gazette, amend the rates specified in the table above.

(2) On payment of the sum of money in accordance with the table above, any person in custody in connection with that offence shall be set at liberty and no proceedings shall be instituted or continued against such person in any court.

(3) The acceptance of the sum of money for compounding an offence in accordance with the table above, by the Court shall be deemed to amount to an acquittal within the meaning of section 300 of the Code of Criminal Procedure, 1973.

(4) The promoter, allottee or real estate agent, as the case may be, shall comply with the orders of the regulatory authority or the Appellate Tribunal, within the period specified by the court, which shall not be more than 30 days from the date of compounding of the offence.

20. Manner of implementation of order, direction or decisions of the adjudicating officer, the Regulatory Authority or the Appellate Tribunal.- For the purpose of sub-section (2) of section 40, every order passed by the Adjudicating Officer, Regulatory Authority or Appellate Tribunal, as the case may be, under the Act or the rules and regulations made thereunder, shall be enforced by the Adjudicating Officer, Regulatory Authority or the Appellate Tribunal in the same manner as if it were a decree or order made by the Principal Civil Court in a suit pending therein and it shall be lawful for the Adjudicating Officer, Regulatory Authority or Appellate Tribunal, as the case may be, in the event of its inability to execute the order, send such order to the Principal Civil Court, to execute such order either within the local limits of whose jurisdiction the real estate project is located or in the Principal Civil Court within the local limits of whose jurisdiction the person against whom the order is being issued, actually and voluntarily resides, or carries on business, or personally works for gain.

Annexure 'A'
Model Form of Agreement to be entered into between
Promoter and Allottee(s) (See rule 9)

EXPLANATORY NOTE

This is a model form of Agreement, which may be modified and adapted in each case having regard to the facts and circumstances of respective case but in any event, matter and substance mentioned in those clauses, which are in accordance with the statute and mandatory according to the provisions of the Act shall be retained in each and every Agreement executed between the Promoter and Allottee. Any clause in this agreement found contrary to or inconsistent with any provisions of the Act, Rules and Regulations would be void *ab-initio*.

Model Form of Agreement

This Agreement made at...........this........day of.......... in the year Two Thousand and.................... between ....having address at ....hereinafter referred to as "the Promoter of the One Part and (.........................) having address at ....hereinafter referred to as " the Allottee" (..........................) of the Other Part.

WHEREAS by an Agreement/Conveyance dated ....day of.... ....20....... and executed between .... of the One Part (hereinafter referred to as " the Vendor") and the Promoter of the Other Part, the Vendor agreed with the Promoter for the absolute sale to the Promoter/sold absolutely to the Promoter an immovable property being piece or parcel of freehold land bearing Survey No. .... lying and being survey no. at .... in the Registration sub-District of .... admeasuring .... sq. mts. or thereabouts more particularly described in the First Schedule hereunder written (hereinafter referred to as "the project land").

OR

WHEREAS by and under a Lease / an Agreement for Lease dated the .... day of.................20....... made between .... of the One Part (hereinafter referred to as " the Lessor") and the Promoter of the Other Part, the Lessor agreed to grant unto the Promoter a lease in perpetuity/for a term of .... years in respect of a piece or parcel of leasehold land bearing situate at ...., admeasuring........sq.m. or thereabouts more particularly described in the First Schedule hereunder written (hereinafter referred to as " the project land") at a rent of Rs........... per annum/month and on the terms and conditions contained in the said Lease
Deed/Agreement for Lease.

AND WHEREAS the lease Deed/Agreement for Lease, is with the benefit and right to construct any new building/s if so permitted by the concerned local authority.

OR

WHEREAS by an Agreement dated ....day of 20......./Power of Attorney dated............. executed between Shri............... (hereinafter referred to as "the Original Owner") of the One Part and the Promoter of the Other Part (hereinafter referred to as "the Development Agreement"), the Original Owner granted to the Promoter development rights to the piece or parcel of freehold land lying and being at .... in the Registration Sub-District of................. admeasuring .... sq. mts., or thereabouts more particularly described in the First Schedule therein as well as in the First Schedule hereunder written (hereinafter referred to as "the project land') and to construct thereon building/s in accordance with the terms and conditions contained in the Development Agreement/Power of Attorney;

OR

(Give Complete Recital of the Title of the Promoter to the plot on which promoter proposes to construct and sale the Apartment)

AND WHEREAS the Promoters are entitled and enjoined upon to construct buildings on the project land;

AND WHEREAS the Vendor/Lessor/Original Owner/Promoter is in possession of the project land

AND WHEREAS the Promoter has proposed to construct on the project land (here specify number of buildings and wings thereof) .... having _____(here specify number of Basements/podiums/stilt and upper floors)

AND WHEREAS the Allottee is offered an Apartment bearing number _____ on the _____ floor, (herein after referred to as the said "Apartment") in the _____ wing of the Building called _____ (herein after referred to as the said "Building") being constructed in the_____phase of the said project, by the Promoter

AND WHEREAS the Promoter has registered the Project under the provisions of the Act with the Real Estate Regulatory Authority at _____ no_____; authenticated copy is attached in Annexure 'B';

AND WHEREAS by virtue of the Development Agreement/Power of Attorney the Promoter has sole and exclusive right to sell the Apartments in the said building/s to be constructed by the Promoter on the project land and to enter into Agreement/s with the allottee(s)/s of the Apartments to receive the sale consideration in respect thereof;

AND WHEREAS on demand from the allottee, the Promoter has given inspection to the Allottee of all the documents of title relating to the project land and the plans, designs and specifications prepared by the Promoter's Architects Messrs................................... and of such other documents as are specified under the Real Estate (Regulation and Development) Act, 2016 (hereinafter referred to as "the said Act") and the Rules and Regulations made thereunder and the Allottee if satisfied in respect of the same;

AND WHEREAS the authenticated copies of Certificate of Title issued by the attorney at law or advocate of the Promoter, authenticated copies of Property card or extract of Village Forms VI and VII and XII or any other relevant revenue record showing the nature of the title of the Promoter to the project land on which the Apartments are constructed or are to be constructed have also been inspected by the Allottee and is satisfied in respect of the same.

AND WHEREAS the authenticated copies of the plans of the Layout as approved by the concerned Local Authority has been inspected by the Allottee.

AND WHEREAS the authenticated copies of the plans of the Layout as proposed by the Promoter and according to which the construction of the buildings and open spaces are proposed to be provided for on the said project has also been inspected by the Allottee,

AND WHEREAS the authenticated copies of the plans and specifications of the Apartment agreed to be purchased by the Allottee has been annexed and marked as Annexure A

AND WHEREAS the Promoter has got some of the approvals from the concerned local authority(s) to the plans, the specifications, elevations, sections and of the said building/s and shall obtain the balance approvals from various authorities from time to time, so as to obtain Building Completion Certificate or Occupancy Certificate of the said Building.

AND WHEREAS while sanctioning the said plans concerned local authority and/or Government has laid down certain terms, conditions, stipulations and restrictions which are to be observed and performed by the Promoter while developing the project land and the said building and upon due observance and performance of which only the completion or occupancy certificate in respect of the said building/s shall be granted by the concerned local authority.

AND WHEREAS the Promoter has accordingly commenced construction of the said building/s in accordance with the said proposed plans.

AND WHEREAS the Allottee has applied to the Promoter for allotment of an Apartment No. .... on .... floor in wing _____ situated in the building No. _____ being constructed in the _____ phase of the said Project,

AND WHEREAS the carpet area of the said Apartment is _____ square meters/square feet and "carpet area" means the net usable floor area of an apartment, excluding the area covered by the external walls, areas under services shafts, exclusive balcony or verandah area and exclusive open terrace area but includes the area covered by the internal partition walls of the apartment.

AND WHEREAS, the Parties relying on the confirmations, representations and assurances of each other to faithfully abide by all the terms, conditions and stipulations contained in this Agreement and all applicable laws, are now willing to enter into this Agreement on the terms and conditions appearing hereinafter;

AND WHEREAS, prior to the execution of these presents the Allottee has paid to the Promoter a sum of Rs..................... (Rupees ....) only, being part payment of the sale consideration of the Apartment agreed to be sold by the Promoter to the Allottee as advance payment or Application Fee (the payment and receipt whereof the Promoter both hereby admit and acknowledge) and the Allottee has agreed to pay to the Promoter the balance of the sale consideration in the manner hereinafter appearing.

AND WHEREAS, under section 13 of the said Act the Promoter is required to execute a written Agreement for sale of said Apartment with the Allottee, being in fact these presents and also to register said Agreement under the Registration Act, 1908.

In accordance with the terms and conditions set out in this Agreement and as mutually agreed upon by and between the Parties, the Promoter hereby agrees to sell and the Allottee hereby agrees to purchase the (Apartment/Plot) and the garage/covered parking(if applicable)

NOW THEREFOR, THIS AGREEMENT WITNESSETH AND IT IS HEREBY AGREED BY AND BETWEEN THE PARTIES HERETO AS FOLLOWS:-

1. The Promoter shall construct the said building/s consisting of .... basement and ground/ stilt, /................. podiums, and .... upper floors on the project land in accordance with the plans, designs and specifications as approved by the concerned local authority from time to time.

   Provided that the Promoter shall have to obtain prior consent in writing of the Allottee in respect of variations or modifications which may adversely affect the Apartment of the Allottee except any alteration or addition required by any Government authorities or due to change in law.

1(a) (i) The Allottee hereby agrees to purchase from the Promoter and the Promoter hereby agrees to sell to the Allottee Apartment No. .... of the type .... of carpet area admeasuring .... sq. metres/ sq. feet on .... floor in the building_____/wing (hereinafter referred to as "the Apartment") for the consideration of Rs. .... including Rs. .... being the proportionate price of the common areas and facilities appurtenant to the premises, the nature, extent and description of the common areas and facilities which are more particularly described in the Second Schedule annexed herewith. (the price of the Apartment including the proportionate price of the common areas and facilities and parking spaces should be shown separately).

(ii) The Allottee hereby agrees to purchase from the Promoter and the Promoter hereby agrees to sell to the Allottee balcony/verandha 1 having area admeasuring ……………..sq.metres/sq.feet forming part of the apartment for the consideration of Rs. _____/-

(iii) The Allottee hereby agrees to purchase from the Promoter and the Promoter hereby agrees to sell to the Allottee balcony/verandha 2 having area admeasuring ………………..sq.metres/sq.feet forming part of the apartment for the consideration Rs. _____/-

(iv) The Allottee hereby agrees to purchase from the Promoter and the Promoter hereby agrees to sell to the Allottee wash area balcony having area admeasuring ……………….sq.meters/sq. Feet forming part of the apartment for the consideration of of Rs. _____/-

(v) The Allottee hereby agrees to purchase from the Promoter and the Promoter hereby agrees to sell to the Allottee open terrace having area admeasuring .... sq.meters/sq. Feet forming part of the apartment for the consideration of of Rs. _____/-

(vi) The Allottee hereby agrees to purchase from the Promoter and the Promoter hereby agrees to sell to the Allottee open parking spaces bearing Nos _____ situated at _____ Basement and/or stilt and /or _____ podium being constructed in the layout for the consideration of Rs_____/-

(vii) The Allottee hereby agrees to purchase from the Promoter and the Promoter hereby agrees to sell to the Allottee covered parking spaces bearing Nos _____ situated at Basement and/or stilt and /or _____ podium being constructed in the layout for the consideration of Rs. _____/-.

1(b) The total aggregate consideration amount for the apartment mentioned herein above from clause 1 a (i) to (vii) is thus Rs._____/-

1(c) The Allottee has paid on or before execution of this agreement a sum of Rs _____ (Rupees _____ only) (not exceeding 10% of the total consideration) as advance payment or application fee and hereby agrees to pay to that Promoter the balance amount of Rs ....(Rupees ....) in the following manner :-

    i. Amount of Rs......../-(........) (not exceeding 30% of the total consideration) to be paid to the Promoter after the execution of Agreement

    ii. Amount of Rs......./-(..........) (not exceeding 45% of the total consideration) to be paid to the Promoter on completion of the Plinth of the building or wing in which the said Apartment is located.

    iii. Amount of Rs....../-(...........) (not exceeding 70% of the total consideration) to be paid to the Promoter on completion of the slabs including podiums and stilts of the building or wing in which the said Apartment is located.

    iv. Amount of Rs......./-(.............) (not exceeding 75% of the total consideration) to be paid to the Promoter on completion of the walls, internal plaster, floorings doors and windows of the said Apartment.

    v. Amount of Rs........./- (...........) (not exceeding 80% of the total consideration) to be paid to the Promoter on completion of the Sanitary fittings, staircases, lift wells, lobbies upto the floor level of the said Apartment.

    vi. Amount of Rs....../-(.....) (not exceeding 85% of the total consideration) to be paid to the Promoter on completion of the external plumbing and external plaster, elevation, terraces with waterproofing, of the building or wing in which the said Apartment is located.

    vii. Amount of Rs......./-(...........) (not exceeding 95% of the total consideration) to be paid to the Promoter on completion of the lifts, water pumps, electrical fittings, electro, mechanical and environment requirements, entrance lobby/s, plinth protection, paving of areas appertain and all other requirements as may be prescribed in the Agreement of sale of the building or wing in which the said Apartment is located.

    viii. Balance Amount of Rs...../-(............) against and at the time of handing over of the possession of the Apartment to the Allottee on or after receipt of occupancy certificate or completion certificate.

1(d) The total price as stated above excludes Taxes (consisting of tax paid or payable by the Promoter by way of Value Added Tax, Service Tax, and Cess or any other similar taxes which may be levied, in connection with the construction of and carrying out the Project payable by the Promoter) up to the date of handing over the possession of the [Apartment/Plot], which shall be separatelytpayable by the Allottee in the manner as may be decided by the Promoter.

1(e) The total price is escalation-free, save and except escalations/increases, due to increase on account of development charges payable to the competent authority and/or any other increase in charges which may be levied or imposed by the competent authority Local Bodies/Government from time to time. The Promoter undertakes and agrees that while raising a demand on the Allottee for increase in development charges, cost, or levies imposed by the competent authorities etc., the Promoter shall enclose the said notification/order/rule/regulation published/issued in that behalf to that effect along with the demand letter being issued to the Allottee, which shall only be applicable on subsequent payments.

1(f) The Promoter may allow, in its sole discretion, a rebate for early payments of equal instalments payable by the Allottee by discounting such early payments @ _____ % per annum for the period by which the respective instalment has been preponed. The provision for allowing rebate and such rate of rebate shall not be subject to any revision/withdrawal, once granted to an Allottee by the Promoter.

1(g) The Promoter shall confirm the final carpet area that has been allotted to the Allottee after the construction of the Building is complete and the occupancy certificate is granted by the competent authority, by furnishing details of the changes, if any, in the carpet area, subject to a variation cap of three percent. The total price payable for the carpet area shall be recalculated upon confirmation by the Promoter. If there is any reduction in the carpet area within the defined limit then Promoter shall refund the excess money paid by Allottee within forty-five days with annual interest at the rate of __%, from the date when such an excess amount was paid by the Allottee. If there is any increase in the carpet area allotted to Allottee, the Promoter shall demand additional amount from the Allottee as per the next milestone of the Payment Plan. All these monetary adjustments shall be made at the same rate per square meter as agreed in Clause 1(a) of this Agreement.

1(h) The Allottee authorizes the Promoter to adjust/appropriate all payments made by him/her under any head(s) of dues against lawful outstanding, if any, in his/her name as the Promoter may in its sole discretion deem fit and the Allottee undertakes not to object/demand/direct the Promoter to adjust his payments in any manner.

Note: Each of the instalments mentioned in the sub clause (ii) and (iii) shall be further subdivided into multiple instalments linked to number of basements/podiums/floors in case of multi-storied building /wing.

2.1 The Promoter hereby agrees to observe, perform and comply with all the terms, conditions, stipulations and restrictions if any, which may have been imposed by the concerned local authority at the time of sanctioning the said plans or thereafter and shall, before handing over possession of the Apartment to the Allottee, obtain from the concerned local authority occupancy and/or completion certificates in respect of the Apartment.

2.2 Time is essence for the Promoter as well as the Allottee. The Promoter shall abide by the time schedule for completing the project and handing over the [Apartment/Plot] to the Allottee and the common areas to the association of the allottees after receiving the occupancy certificate or the completion certificate or both, as the case may be.

Similarly, the Allottee shall make timely payments of the instalment and other dues payable by him/her and meeting the other obligations under the Agreement subject to the simultaneous completion of construction by the Promoter as provided in clause 1 (c) herein above. ("Payment Plan").

3. The Promoter hereby declares that the Floor Space Index available as on date in respect of the project land is .... square meters only and Promoter has planned to utilize Floor Space Index of _____ by availing of TDR or FSI available on payment of premiums or FSI available as incentive FSI by implementing various scheme as mentioned in the Development Control Regulation or based on expectation of increased FSI which may be available in future on modification to Development Control Regulations, which are applicable to the said Project. The Promoter has disclosed the Floor Space Index of _____ as proposed to be utilized by him on the project land in the said Project and Allottee has agreed to purchase the said Apartment based on the proposed construction and sale of apartments to be carried out by the Promoter by utilizing the proposed FSI and on the understanding that the declared proposed FSI shall belong to Promoter only.

4.1 If the Promoter fails to abide by the time schedule for completing the project and handing over the [Apartment/Plot] to the Allottee, the Promoter agrees to pay to the Allottee, who does not intend to withdraw from the project, interest at the rate of __% per annum, on all the amounts paid by the Allottee, for every month of delay, till the handing over of the possession. The Allottee agrees to pay to the Promoter, interest at the rate of __% per annum, on all the delayed payment which become due and payable by the Allottee to the Promoter under the terms of this Agreement from the date the said amount is payable by the allottee(s) to the Promoter.

4.2 Without prejudice to the right of promoter to charge interest in terms of sub clause 4.1 above, on the Allottee committing default in payment on due date of any amount due and payable by the Allottee to the Promoter under this Agreement (including his/her proportionate share of taxes levied by concerned local authority and other outgoings) and on the allottee committing three defaults of payment of instalments, the Promoter shall at his own option, may terminate this Agreement:

Provided that, Promoter shall give notice of fifteen days in writing to the Allottee, by Registered Post AD at the address provided by the allottee and mail at the e-mail address provided by the Allottee, of his intention to terminate this Agreement and of the specific breach or breaches of terms and conditions in respect of which it is intended to terminate the Agreement. If the Allottee fails to rectify the breach or breaches mentioned by the Promoter within the period of notice then at the end of such notice period, promoter shall be entitled to terminate this Agreement.

Provided further that upon termination of this Agreement as aforesaid, the Promoter shall refund to the Allottee (subject to adjustment and recovery of any agreed liquidated damages or any other amount which may be payable to Promoter) within a period of thirty days of the termination, the instalments of sale consideration of the Apartment which may till then have been paid by the Allottee to the Promoter.

5. The fixtures and fittings with regard to the flooring and sanitary fittings and amenities like one or more lifts with brand, or price range to be provided by the Promoter at his/her/its option in the said building and the Apartment as are set out in Annexure 'C', annexed hereto.

6. The Promoter shall give possession of the Apartment to the Allottee on or before................. day of ....20___. If the Promoter fails or neglects to give possession of the Apartment to the Allottee on account of reasons beyond his control and of his agents by the aforesaid date then the Promoter shall be liable on demand to refund to the Allottee the amounts already received by him in respect of the Apartment with interest at the same rate as may mentioned in the clause 4.1 herein above from the date the Promoter received the sum till the date the amounts and interest thereon is repaid.

Provided that the Promoter shall be entitled to reasonable extension of time for giving delivery of Apartment on the aforesaid date, if the completion of building in which the Apartment is to be situated is delayed on account of -
    (i)   war, civil commotion or act of God ;
    (ii)   any notice, order, rule, notification of the Government and/or other public or competent authority/court.

7.1 **Procedure for taking possession** - The Promoter, upon obtaining the occupancy certificate from the competent authority and the payment made by the Allottee as per the agreement shall offer in writing the possession of the [Apartment/Plot], to the Allottee in terms of this Agreement to be taken within 3 (three months from the date of issue of such notice and the Promoter shall give possession of the [Apartment/Plot] to the Allottee. The Promoter agrees and undertakes to indemnify the Allottee in case of failure of fulfilment of any of the provisions, formalities, documentation on part of the Promoter. The Allottee agree(s) to pay the maintenance charges as determined by the Promoter or association of allottees, as the case may be. The Promoter on its behalf shall offer the possession to the Allottee in writing within 7 days of receiving the occupancy certificate of the Project.

7.2 The Allottee shall take possession of the Apartment within 15 days of the written notice from the promotor to the Allottee intimating that the said Apartments are ready for use and occupancy:

7.3 **Failure of Allottee to take Possession of [Apartment/Plot]:** Upon receiving a written intimation from the Promoter as per clause 7.1, the Allottee shall take possession of the [Apartment/Plot] from the Promoter by executing necessary indemnities, undertakings and such other documentation as prescribed in this Agreement, and the Promoter shall give possession of the [Apartment/Plot] to the allottee. In case the Allottee fails to take possession within the time provided in clause 7.1 such Allottee shall continue to be liable to pay maintenance charges as applicable.

7.4 If within a period of five years from the date of handing over the Apartment to the Allottee, the Allottee brings to the notice of the Promoter any structural defect in the Apartment or the building in which the Apartment are situated or any defects on account of workmanship, quality or provision of service, then, wherever possible such defects shall be rectified by the Promoter at his own cost and in case it is not possible to rectify such defects, then the Allottee shall be entitled to receive from the Promoter, compensation for such defect in the manner as provided under the Act. Provided that the Promoter shall not be liable in respect of any structural defect or defects on account of workmanship, quality or provision of service which cannot be attributable to the Promoter or beyond the control of the Promoter.

8. The Allottee shall use the Apartment or any part thereof or permit the same to be used only for purpose of *residence/office/show-room/shop/godown for carrying on any industry or business.(*strike of which is not applicable) He shall use the garage or parking space only for purpose of keeping or parking vehicle.

9. The Allottee along with other allottee(s)s of Apartments in the building shall join in forming and registering the Society or Association or a Limited Company to be known by such name as the Promoter may decide and for this purpose also from time to time sign and execute the application for registration and/or membership and the other papers and documents necessary for the formation and registration of the Society or Association or Limited Company and for becoming a member, including the bye-laws of the proposed Society and duly fill in, sign and return to the Promoter within seven days of the same being forwarded by the Promoter to the Allottee, so as to enable the Promoter to register the common organisation of Allottee. No objection shall be taken by the Allottee if any, changes or modifications are made in the draft bye-laws, or the Memorandum and/or Articles of Association, as may be required by the Registrar of Co-operative Societies or the Registrar of Companies, as the case may be, or any other Competent Authority.

9.1 Within 15 days after notice in writing is given by the Promoter to the Allottee that the Apartment is ready for use and occupancy, the Allottee shall be liable to bear and pay the proportionate share (i.e. in proportion to the carpet area of the Apartment) of outgoings in respect of the project land and Building/s namely local taxes, betterment charges or such other levies by the concerned local authority and/or Government, water charges, insurance, common lights, repairs and salaries of clerks bill collectors, chowkidars, sweepers and all other expenses necessary and incidental to the management and maintenance of the project land and building/s. Until the Society or Limited Company is formed, the Allottee shall pay to the Promoter such proportionate share of outgoings as may be determined. The Allottee further agrees that till the Allottee's share is so determined the Allottee shall pay to the Promoter provisional monthly contribution of Rs. .... per month towards the outgoings. The amounts so paid by the Allottee to the Promoter shall not carry any interest and remain with the Promoter until the same is transferred to the society or the association or the limited company as aforesaid.

10. Over and above the amounts mentioned in the agreement to be paid by the Allottee, the Allottee shall on or before delivery of possession of the said premises shall pay to the Promoter such proportionate share of the outgoings as may be determined by the Promoter and which are not covered in any other provisions of this agreement.

11. The Allottee shall pay to the Promoter a sum of Rs. .... for meeting all legal costs, charges and expenses, including professional costs of the Attorney-at-Law/Advocates of the Promoter in connection with formation of the said Society, or Limited Company, or Apex Body or Federation and for preparing its rules, regulations and bye-laws and the cost of preparing and engrossing the conveyance or assignment of lease.

12. At the time of registration of conveyance or Lease of the structure of the building or wing of the building, the Allottee shall pay to the Promoter, the Allottees' share of stamp duty and registration charges payable, by the said Society or Limited Company on such conveyance or lease or any

document or instrument of transfer in respect of the structure of the said Building /wing of the building. At the time of registration of conveyance or Lease of the project land, the Allottee shall pay to the Promoter, the Allottees' share of stamp duty and registration charges payable, by the said Apex Body or Federation on such conveyance or lease or any document or instrument of transfer in respect of the structure of the said land to be executed in favour of the Apex Body or Federation.

13. REPRESENTATIONS AND WARRANTIES OF THE PROMOTER
    The Promoter hereby represents and warrants to the Allottee as follows:

    i. The Promoter has clear and marketable title with respect to the project land; as declared in the title report annexed to this agreement and has the requisite rights to carry out development upon the project land and also has actual, physical and legal possession of the project land for the implementation of the Project;
    ii. The Promoter has lawful rights and requisite approvals from the competent Authorities to carry out development of the Project and shall obtain requisite approvals from time to time to complete the development of the project;
    iii. There are no encumbrances upon the project land or the Project except those disclosed in the title report;
    iv. There are no litigations pending before any Court of law with respect to the project land or Project except those disclosed in the title report;
    v. All approvals, licenses and permits issued by the competent authorities with respect to the Project, project land and said building/wing are valid and subsisting and have been obtained by following due process of law. Further, all approvals, licenses and permits to be issued by the competent authorities with respect to the Project, project land and said building/wing shall be obtained by following due process of law and the Promoter has been and shall, at all times, remain to be in compliance with all applicable laws in relation to the Project, project land, Building/wing and common areas;
    vi. The Promoter has the right to enter into this Agreement and has not committed or omitted to perform any act or thing, whereby the right, title and interest of the Allottee created herein, may prejudicially be affected;
    vii. The Promoter has not entered into any agreement for sale and/or development agreement or any other agreement / arrangement with any person or party with respect to the project land, including the Project and the said [Apartment/Plot] which will, in any manner, affect the rights of Allottee under this Agreement;
    viii. The Promoter confirms that the Promoter is not restricted in any manner whatsoever from selling the said [Apartment/Plot] to the Allottee in the manner contemplated in this Agreement;
    ix. At the time of execution of the conveyance deed of the structure to the association of allottees the Promoter shall handover lawful, vacant, peaceful, physical possession of the common areas of the Structure to the Association of the Allottees;
    x. The Promoter has duly paid and shall continue to pay and discharge undisputed governmental dues, rates, charges and taxes and other monies, levies, impositions, premiums, damages and/or penalties and other outgoings, whatsoever, payable with respect to the said project to the competent Authorities;
    xi. No notice from the Government or any other local body or authority or any legislative enactment, government ordinance, order, notification (including any notice for acquisition or requisition of the said property) has been received or served upon the Promoter in respect of the project land and/or the Project except those disclosed in the title report.

14. The Allottee/s or himself/themselves with intention to bring all persons into whosoever hands the Apartment may come, hereby covenants with the Promoter as follows :-
    i. To maintain the Apartment at the Allottee's own cost in good and tenantable repair and condition from the date that of possession of the Apartment is taken and shall not do or suffer to be done anything in or to the building in which the Apartment is situated which may be against the rules, regulations or bye-laws or change/alter or make addition in or to the building in which the Apartment is situated and the Apartment itself or any part thereof without the consent of the local authorities, if required.
    ii. Not to store in the Apartment any goods which are of hazardous, combustible or dangerous nature or are so heavy as to damage the construction or structure of the building in which the Apartment is situated or storing of which goods is objected to by the concerned local or other authority and shall take care while carrying heavy packages which may damage or likely to damage the staircases, common passages or any other structure of the building in which the Apartment is situated, including entrances of the building in which the Apartment is situated and in case any damage is caused to the building in which the Apartment is situated or the Apartment on account of negligence or default of the Allottee in this behalf, the Allottee shall be liable for the consequences of the breach.
    iii. To carry out at his own cost all internal repairs to the said Apartment and maintain the Apartment in the same condition, state and order in which it was delivered by the Promoter to the Allottee and shall not do or suffer to be done anything in or to the building in which the Apartment is situated or the Apartment which may be contrary to the rules and regulations and bye-laws of the concerned local authority or other public authority. In the event of the Allottee committing any act in contravention of the above provision, the Allottee shall be responsible and liable for the consequences thereof to the concerned local authority and/or other public authority.
    iv. Not to demolish or cause to be demolished the Apartment or any part thereof, nor at any time make or cause to be made any addition or alteration of whatever nature in or to the Apartment or any part thereof, nor any alteration in the elevation and outside colour scheme of the building in which the Apartment is situated and shall keep the portion, sewers, drains and pipes in the Apartment and the appurtenances thereto in good tenantable repair and condition, and in particular, so as to support shelter and protect the other parts of the building in which the Apartment is situated and shall not chisel or in any other manner cause damage to columns, beams, walls, slabs or RCC, Pardis or other structural members in the Apartment without the prior written permission of the Promoter and/or the Society or the Limited Company.
    v. Not to do or permit to be done any act or thing which may render void or voidable any insurance of the project land and the building in which the Apartment is situated or any part thereof or whereby any increased premium shall become payable in respect of the insurance.
    vi. Not to throw dirt, rubbish, rags, garbage or other refuse or permit the same to be thrown from the said Apartment in the compound or any portion of the project land and the building in which the Apartment is situated.
    vii. Pay to the Promoter within fifteen days of demand by the Promoter, his share of security deposit demanded by the concerned local authority or Government or giving water, electricity or any other service connection to the building in which the Apartment is situated.

viii. To bear and pay increase in local taxes, water charges, insurance and such other levies, if any, which are imposed by the concerned local authority and/or Government and/or other public authority, on account of change of user of the Apartment by the Allottee for any purposes other than for purpose for which it is sold.

ix. The Allottee shall not let, sub-let, transfer, assign or part with interest or benefit factor of this Agreement or part with the possession of the Apartment until all the dues payable by the Allottee to the Promoter under this Agreement are fully paid up.

x. The Allottee shall observe and perform all the rules and regulations which the Society or the Limited Company or Apex Body or Federation may adopt at its inception and the additions, alterations or amendments thereof that may be made from time to time for protection and maintenance of the said building and the Apartments therein and for the observance and performance of the Building Rules, Regulations and Bye-laws for the time being of the concerned local authority and of Government and other public bodies. The Allottee shall also observe and perform all the stipulations and conditions laid down by the Society/Limited Company/Apex Body/Federation regarding the occupancy and use of the Apartment in the Building and shall pay and contribute regularly and punctually towards the taxes, expenses or other out-goings in accordance with the terms of this Agreement.

xi. The Allottee shall permit the Promoter and their surveyors and agents, with or without workmen and others, at all reasonable times, to enter into and upon the said buildings or any part thereof to view and examine the state and condition thereof.

xii. The Allottee shall permit the Promoter and their surveyors and agents, with or without workmen and others, at all reasonable times, to enter into and upon the project land or any part thereof to view and examine the state and condition thereof.

15. The Promoter shall maintain a separate account in respect of sums received by the Promoter from the Allottee as advance or deposit, sums received on account of the share capital for the promotion of the Co-operative Society or association or Company or towards the out goings, legal charges and shall utilize the amounts only for the purposes for which they have been received.

16. Nothing contained in this Agreement is intended to be nor shall be construed as a grant, demise or assignment in law, of the said Apartments or of the said Plot and Building or any part thereof. The Allottee shall have no claim save and except in respect of the Apartment hereby agreed to be sold to him and all open spaces, parking spaces, lobbies, staircases, terraces recreation spaces, will remain the property of the Promoter until the same is transferred as hereinbefore mentioned.

17. PROMOTER SHALL NOT MORTGAGE OR CREATE A CHARGE

After the Promoter executes this Agreement he shall not mortgage or create a charge on the *[Apartment/] and if any such mortgage or charge is made or created then notwithstanding anything contained in any other law for the time being in force, such mortgage or charge shall not affect the right and interest of the Allottee who has taken or agreed to take such [Apartment/plot].

18. BINDING EFFECT

Forwarding this Agreement to the Allottee by the Promoter does not create a binding obligation on the part of the Promoter or the Allottee until, firstly, the Allottee signs and delivers this Agreement with all the schedules along with the payments due as stipulated in the Payment Plan within 30 (thirty) days from the date of receipt by the Allottee and secondly, appears for registration of the same before the concerned Sub- Registrar as and when intimated by the Promoter. If the

Allottee(s) fails to execute and deliver to the Promoter this Agreement within 30 (thirty) days from the date of its receipt by the Allottee and/or appear before the Sub-Registrar for its registration as and when intimated by the Promoter, then the Promoter shall serve a notice to the Allottee for rectifying the default, which if not rectified within 15 (fifteen) days from the date of its receipt by the Allottee, application of the Allottee shall be treated as cancelled and all sums deposited by the Allottee in connection therewith including the booking amount shall be returned to the Allottee without any interest or compensation whatsoever.

19. ENTIRE AGREEMENT

This Agreement, along with its schedules and annexures, constitutes the entire Agreement between the Parties with respect to the subject matter hereof and supersedes any and all understandings, any other agreements, allotment letter, correspondences, arrangements whether written or oral, if any, between the Parties in regard to the said apartment/plot/building, as the case may be.

20. RIGHT TO AMEND

This Agreement may only be amended through written consent of the Parties.

21. PROVISIONS OF THIS AGREEMENT APPLICABLE TO ALLOTTEE/ SUBSEQUENT ALLOTTEES

It is clearly understood and so agreed by and between the Parties hereto that all the provisions contained herein and the obligations arising hereunder in respect of the Project shall equally be applicable to and enforceable against any subsequent Allottees of the [Apartment/Plot], in case of a transfer, as the said obligations go along with the [Apartment/Plot] for all intents and purposes.

22. SEVERABILITY

If any provision of this Agreement shall be determined to be void or unenforceable under the Act or the Rules and Regulations made thereunder or under other applicable laws, such provisions of the Agreement shall be deemed amended or deleted in so far as reasonably inconsistent with the purpose of this Agreement and to the extent necessary to conform to Act or the Rules and Regulations made thereunder or the applicable law, as the case may be, and the remaining provisions of this Agreement shall remain valid and enforceable as applicable at the time of execution of this Agreement.

23. METHOD OF CALCULATION OF PROPORTIONATE SHARE WHEREVER REFERRED TO IN THE AGREEMENT

Wherever in this Agreement it is stipulated that the Allottee has to make any payment, in common with other Allottee(s) in Project, the same shall be in proportion to the carpet area of the [Apartment/Plot] to the total carpet area of all the [Apartments/Plots] in the Project.

24. FURTHER ASSURANCES

Both Parties agree that they shall execute, acknowledge and deliver to the other such instruments and take such other actions, in additions to the instruments and actions specifically provided for herein, as may be reasonably required in order to effectuate the provisions of this Agreement or of any transaction contemplated herein or to confirm or perfect any right to be created or transferred hereunder or pursuant to any such transaction.

25. PLACE OF EXECUTION

The execution of this Agreement shall be complete only upon its execution by the Promoter through its authorized signatory at the Promoter's Office, or at some other place, which may be mutually agreed between the Promoter and the Allottee, in _____after the Agreement is duly executed by the Allottee and the Promoter or simultaneously with the execution the said Agreement shall be registered at the office of the Sub-Registrar. Hence this Agreement shall be deemed to have been executed at_____.

26. The Allottee and/or Promoter shall present this Agreement as well as the conveyance/assignment of lease at the proper registration office of registration within the time limit prescribed by the Registration Act and the Promoter will attend such office and admit execution thereof.

27. That all notices to be served on the Allottee and the Promoter as contemplated by this Agreement shall be deemed to have been duly served if sent to the Allottee or the Promoter by Registered Post A.D and notified Email ID/Under Certificate of Posting at their respective addresses specified below:

_____Name of Allottee
_____(Allottee's Address) Notified Email ID:_____

M/s_____Promoter name
_____(Promoter Address) Notified Email ID:_____

It shall be the duty of the Allottee and the promoter to inform each other of any change in address subsequent to the execution of this Agreement in the above address by Registered Post failing which all communications and letters posted at the above address shall be deemed to have been received by the promoter or the Allottee, as the case may be.

28. JOINT ALLOTTEES
That in case there are Joint Allottees all communications shall be sent by the Promoter to the Allottee whose name appears first and at the address given by him/her which shall for all intents and purposes to consider as properly served on all the Allottees.

29. Stamp Duty and Registration:- The charges towards stamp duty and Registration of this Agreement shall be borne by the allottee.

30. Dispute Resolution:- Any dispute between parties shall be settled amicably. In case of failure to settled the dispute amicably, which shall be referred to the _____ Authority as per the provisions of the Real Estate (Regulation and Development) Act, 2016, Rules and Regulations, thereunder.

31. GOVERNING LAW
That the rights and obligations of the parties under or arising out of this Agreement shall be construed and enforced in accordance with the laws of India for the time being in force and the _____ courts will have the jurisdiction for this Agreement

IN WITNESS WHEREOF parties hereinabove named have set their respective hands and signed this Agreement for sale at_____(city/town name) in the presence of attesting witness, signing as such on the day first above written.

First Schedule Above Referred to Description of the freehold/leasehold land and all other details.

Second Schedule Above Referred to here set out the nature, extent and description of common areas and facilities.

SIGNED AND DELIVERED BY THE WITHIN NAMED

Allottee: (including joint buyers)

Please affix photograph and sign across the photograph	Please affix photograph and sign across the photograph

(1)_____

(2)_____

At_____on_____

in the presence of WITNESSES:

1. Name _____
   Signature _____

2. Name _____
   Signature _____

SIGNED AND DELIVERED BY THE WITHIN NAMED

Promoter:

(1)_____

(Authorized Signatory) WITNESSES:

| Please affix photograph and sign across the photograp |

Name _____

Signature _____

Name _____

Signature _____

Note – Execution clauses to be finalised in individual cases having regard to the constitution of the parties to the Agreement.

SCHEDULE 'A'

PLEASE INSERT DESCRIPTION OF THE [APARTMENT/PLOT] AND THE GARAGE/CLOSED PARKING (IF APPLICABLE) ALONG WITH BOUNDARIES IN ALL FOUR DIRECTIONS

SCHEDULE 'B'
FLOOR PLAN OF THE APARTMENT

ANNEXURE -A

(Authenticated copies of the plans and specifications of the Apartment agreed to be purchased by the Allottee as approved by the concerned local authority)

ANNEXURE –B

(Authenticated copy of the Registration Certificate of the Project granted by the Real Estate Regulatory Authority)

ANNEXURE – C

(Specification and amenities for the Apartment)

Received of and from the Allottee above named the sum of Rupees .... on execution of this agreement towards Earnest Money Deposit or application fee I say received.

The Promoter/s.

FORM 'A'
[See rule 3(2)]

APPLICATION FOR REGISTRATION OF PROJECT

To

    The Real Estate Regulatory Authority

    _____

    _____

Sir,

    I/We hereby apply for the grant of registration of my/our project to be set up at _____ Tehsil _____ District _____ State _____.

1. The requisite particulars are as under:-
(i) Status of the applicant, whether individual / company / proprietorship firm / societies / partnership firm / competent authority;
(ii) In case of individual –
    (a) Name
    (b) Father's Name
    (c) Occupation
    (d) Permanent address
    (e) Photograph

OR

In case of firm / societies / trust / companies / limited liability partnership / competent authority -
    (a) Name
    (b) Address
    (c) Copy of registration certificate
    (d) Main objects
    (e) Name, photograph and address of chairman of the governing body / partners / directors etc.

(iii) PAN No. _____;
(iv) Name and address of the bank or banker with which account in terms of section 4 (2)(l)(D) of the Act will be maintained _____;
(v) Details of project land held by the applicant _____;
(vi) brief details of the projects launched by the promoter in the last five years, whether already completed or being developed, as the case may be, including the current status of the said projects, any delay in its completion, details of cases pending, details of type of land and payments pending etc._____;
(vii) Agency to take up external development works _____ Local Authority / Self Development;
(viii) Registration fee by way of a demand draft dated _____ drawn on _____ bearing no. _____ for an amount of Rs._____/- calculated as per sub-rule (3) of rule 3;
(ix) Any other information the applicant may like to furnish.

2. I/we enclose the following documents in triplicate, namely:-
   (i) authenticated copy of the PAN card of the promoter;
   (ii) audited balance sheet of the promoter for the preceding financial year and income tax returns of the promoter for three preceding financial years;
   (iii) copy of the legal title deed reflecting the title of the promoter to the land on which development is proposed to be developed along with legally valid documents with authentication of such title, if such land is owned by another person;
   (iv) the details of encumbrances on the land on which development is proposed including any rights, title, interest or name of any party in or over such land along with details;
   (v) where the promoter is not the owner of the land on which development is proposed details of the consent of the owner of the land along with a copy of the collaboration agreement, development agreement, joint development agreement or any other agreement, as the case may be, entered into between the promoter and such owner and copies of title and other documents reflecting the title of such owner on the land proposed to be developed;
   (vi) an authenticated copy of the approvals and commencement certificate from the competent authority obtained in accordance with the laws as may be applicable for the for the real estate project mentioned in the application, and where the project is proposed to be developed in phases, an authenticated copy of the approvals and commencement certificate from the competent authority for each of such phases;
   (vii) the sanctioned plan, layout plan and specifications of the proposed project or the phase thereof, and the whole project as sanctioned by the competent authority;
   (viii) the plan of development works to be executed in the proposed project and the proposed facilities to be provided thereof including fire-fighting facilities, drinking water facilities, emergency evacuation services, use of renewable energy;
   (ix) the location details of the project, with clear demarcation of land dedicated for the project along with its boundaries including the latitude and longitude of the end points of the project;
   (x) proforma of the allotment letter, agreement for sale, and the conveyance deed proposed to be signed with the allottees;
   (xi) the number, type and the carpet area of apartments for sale in the project along with the area of the exclusive balcony or verandah areas and the exclusive open terrace areas apartment with the apartment, if any;
   (xii) the number and areas of garage for sale in the project;
   (xiii) the number of open parking areas available in the real estate project;
   (xiv) the names and addresses of the real estate agents, if any, for the proposed project;
   (xv) the names and addresses of the contractors, architect, structural engineer, if any and other persons concerned with the development of the proposed project;
   (xvi) a declaration in FORM 'B'.

3. I/We solemnly affirm and declare that the particulars given in herein are correct to my/our knowledge and belief.

Dated: Place:

Yours faithfully,
Signature and seal of the applicant(s)

FORM 'B'
[See rule 3(4)]

DECLARATION, SUPPORTED BY AN AFFIDAVIT, WHICH SHALL BE SIGNED BY THE PROMOTER OR ANY PERSON AUTHORIZED BY THE PROMOTER

Affidavit cum Declaration

Affidavit cum Declaration of Mr./Ms. _____ promoter of the proposed project / duly authorized by the promoter of the proposed project, vide its/his/their authorization dated _____;

I, _____ promoter of the proposed project / duly authorized by the promoter of the proposed project do hereby solemnly declare, undertake and state as under:

1. That I / promoter have / has a legal title to the land on which the development of the project is proposed

OR

_____ have/has a legal title to the land on which the development of the proposed project is to be carried out

AND

a legally valid authentication of title of such land along with an authenticated copy of the agreement between such owner and promoter for development of the real estate project is enclosed herewith.

2. That the said land is free from all encumbrances.

OR

That details of encumbrances _____ including details of any rights, title, interest or name of any party in or over such land, along with details.

3. That the time period within which the project shall be completed by me/promoter is _____.

4. That seventy per cent of the amounts realised by me/promoter for the real estate project from the allottees, from time to time, shall be deposited in a separate account to be maintained in a scheduled bank to cover the cost of construction and the land cost and shall be used only for that purpose.

5. That the amounts from the separate account, to cover the cost of the project, shall be withdrawn in proportion to the percentage of completion of the project.

6. That the amounts from the separate account shall be withdrawn after it is certified by an engineer, an architect and a chartered accountant in practice that the withdrawal is in proportion to the percentage of completion of the project.

7. That I/promoter shall get the accounts audited within six months after the end of every financial year by a chartered accountant in practice, and shall produce a statement of accounts duly certified and signed by such chartered accountant and it shall be verified during the audit that the amounts collected for a particular project have been utilised for the project and the withdrawal has been in compliance with the proportion to the percentage of completion of the project.

8. That I/promoter shall take all the pending approvals on time, from the competent authorities.

9. That I/promoter have / has furnished such other documents as have been prescribed by the rules and regulations made under the Act.

Deponent

Verification

The contents of my above Affidavit cum Declaration are true and correct and nothing material has been concealed by me therefrom.

Verify by me at _____ on this _____ day of _____ .

Deponent

FORM 'C'
[See rule 6(1)]

REGISTRATION CERTIFICATE OF PROJECT

This registration is granted under section 5 of the Act to the following project under project registration number _____ :

_____
(Specify Details of Project including the project address);

1.   (in the case of an individual) Mr./Ms. _____ son of Mr./Ms._____ Tehsil_____ District_____State_____;

OR

    (in the case of a firm / society / company / competent authority) _____ firm/society/company/competent authority _____ having its registered office / principal place of business at _____.

2. This registration is granted subject to the following conditions, namely:-

    (i) The promoter shall enter into an agreement for sale with the allottees as provided in 'Annexure A';
    (ii) The promoter shall execute and register a conveyance deed in favour of the allottee or the association of the allottees, as the case may be, of the apartment or the common areas in accordance with the section 17;
    (iii) The promoter shall deposit seventy percent of the amounts realised by the promoter in a separate account to be maintained in a schedule bank to cover the cost of construction and the land cost to be used only for that purpose in accordance with the sub- clause (D) of clause (l) of sub-section (2) of section 4;
    (iv) The registration shall be valid for a period of _____ years commencing from _____ and ending with _____ unless renewed by the Real Estate Regulatory Authority in accordance with section 6 read with rule 7 of the Act;
    (v) The promoter shall comply with the provisions of the Act and the rules and regulations made thereunder;
    (vi) The promoter shall not contravene the provisions of any other law for the time being in force in the area where the project is being developed.

3. If the above mentioned conditions are not fulfilled by the promoter, the regulatory authority may take necessary action against the promoter including revoking the registration granted herein, in accordance with the Act and the rules and regulations made thereunder.

Dated:
Place:

Signature and seal of the Authorized Officer
Real Estate Regulatory Authority

FORM 'D'
[See rule 6(2), rule 7; rule 8]

INTIMATION OF REJECTION OF APPLICATION FOR REGISTRATION OF PROJECT / REJECTION OF APPLICATION FOR EXTENSION OF REGISTRATION OF PROJECT / REVOCATION OF REGISTRATION OF PROJECT

From:

    The Real Estate Regulatory Authority,

    ………………………………………..

    ………………………………………..

To

    ………………………………………..

    ………………………………………..

    ………………………………………..

    Application/Registration No.: ……………………
    Dated:……………………..

You are hereby informed that your application for registration of your project is rejected.

OR

You are hereby informed that your application for extension of the registration of your project is rejected.

OR

You are hereby informed that the registration granted to your project is hereby revoked.

for the reasons set out:- _____

Place:
Dated:

Signature and seal of the Authorized Officer
Real Estate Regulatory Authority

FORM 'E'
[See rule 7(1)]

APPLICATION FOR EXTENSION OF REGISTRATION OF PROJECT

From:

....

....

....

To

The Real Estate Regulatory Authority,

....

....

....

Sir,

I/We hereby apply for renewal of registration of the following project:

....
....
registered with the regulatory authority vide project registration certificate bearing No. ...., which expires on ....

As required I/we submit the following documents and information, namely:-

(i) A demand Draft No. .... dated .... for rupees .... in favour of ....drawn on .... bank as extension fee as provided under sub-rule (2) of rule 7;

(ii) Authenticated Plan of the project showing the stage of development works undertaken till date;

(iii) Explanatory note regarding the state of development works in the project and reason for not completing the development works in the project within the period declared in the declaration submitted in Form 'B' at the time of making application for the registration of the project ....;

(iv) Authenticated copy of the permission/approval from the competent authority which is valid for a period which is longer than the proposed term of extension of the registration sought from the regulatory authority;

(v) The original project registration certificate; and

(vi) Any other information as may be specified by regulations.

Place:
Dated:

Yours faithfully,
Signature and seal of the applicant(s)

FORM 'F'
[See rule 7(2)]

CERTIFICATE FOR EXTENSION OF REGISTRATION OF PROJECT

This extension of registration is granted under section 6 of the Act, to the following project: ………………………………………………………………………………………… ………………………………………………………………………………………… registered with the regulatory authority vide project registration certificate bearing No. …………………………………… of

1. (in the case of an individual) Mr./Ms. ……………………………………… son of Mr./Ms. ………………………………… Tehsil …………… District ………………… State ………………;

    OR

    (in the case of a firm / society / company / competent authority) …………………… firm / society / company / competent authority ………………….. having its registered office/principal place of business at ……………………..

2. This renewal of registration is granted subject to the following conditions, namely:-

    (i) The promoter shall execute and register a conveyance deed in favour of the allottee or the association of the allottees, as the case may be, of the apartment or the common areas in accordance with the section 17;

    (ii) The promoter shall deposit seventy percent of the amounts realised by the promoter in a separate account to be maintained in a schedule bank to cover the cost of construction and the land cost to be used only for that purpose in accordance with the sub-clause (D) of clause (l) of sub-section (2) of section 4;

    (iii) The registration shall be valid for a period of …………. years commencing from …………. and ending with ……………………… unless renewed by the Real Estate Regulatory Authority in accordance with section 6 read with section 7 of the Act;

    (iv) The promoter shall comply with the provisions of the Act and the rules and regulations made thereunder;

    (v) The promoter shall not contravene the provisions of any other law for the time being in force in the area where the project is being developed;

    (vi) If the above mentioned conditions are not fulfilled by the promoter, the regulatory authority may take necessary action against the promoter including revoking the registration granted herein, in accordance with the Act and the rules and regulations made thereunder.

Dated:
Place:

Signature and seal of the Authorized Officer
Real Estate Regulatory Authority

FORM 'G'
[See rule 10(1)]

APPLICATION FOR REGISTRATION OF REAL ESTATE AGENT

To

The Real Estate Regulatory Authority

…………………………………….

…………………………………….

Sir,

I/We beg to apply for the grant of registration as a real estate agent to facilitate the sale or purchase of any plot, apartment or building, as the case may be, in real estate projects registered in the ………… State in terms of the Act and the rules and regulations made thereunder,

1. (in the case of an individual) Mr./Ms. ……………………………………. son of Mr./Ms. …………………………………. Tehsil …………… District ……………. State ……………..;

OR

(in the case of a firm / society / company) ……………………. firm / society / company ………………….. having its registered office/principal place of business at ……………………..

2. The requisite particulars are as under:-

   (i) Status of the applicant, whether individual / company / proprietorship firm / societies / partnership firm / limited liability partnership;

   (ii) In case of individual –
   - (a) Name
   - (b) Father's Name
   - (c) Occupation
   - (d) Permanent address
   - (e) Photograph

   OR

   In case of firm / societies / companies –
   - (a) Name
   - (b) Address
   - (c) Copy of registration certificate
   - (d) Major activities
   - (e) Name, photograph and address of partners / directors etc.

(iii) income tax returns filed under the provisions of the Income Tax Act, 1961 for three financial years preceding the application or in case the applicant was exempted from filing returns under the provisions of the Income Tax Act, 1961 for any of the three year preceding the application, a declaration to such effects;

(iv) particulars of registration including the bye-laws, memorandum of association, articles of association etc. as the case may be;

(v) authenticated copy of the address proof of the place of business;

(vi) Details of registration in any other State or Union territory;

(vii) Any other information the applicant may like to furnish.

3. I/we enclose the following documents along with, namely:-

(i) Demand Draft No. ………………… dated ………………… for a sum of Rs. …………………, in favour of …………………, drawn on ………………… bank as registration fee in accordance with the sub-rule (2) of rule 10;

(ii) Income tax returns of the last 3 years or declaration as the case may be;

(iii) authenticated copy of the PAN card of the real estate agent; and

(iv) authenticated copy of the registration as a real estate agent in any other State or Union territory, if applicable;

4. I/we solemnly affirm and declare that the particulars given in herein are correct to my /our knowledge and belief.

Dated:
Place:

Yours faithfully,
Signature and seal of the applicant(s)

FORM 'H'
[See rule 11(1)]

REGISTRATION CERTIFICATE OF REAL ESTATE AGENT

1. This registration is granted under section 9 of the Act with registration certificate bearing No. ……………………… to -

    (in the case of an individual) Mr./Ms. ………………………………………… son of Mr./Ms. ………………………………… Tehsil …………… District ……………… State ……………;

    OR

    (in the case of a firm / society / company) …………………… firm / society / company ………………….. having its registered office/principal place of business at ……………………..

    to act as a real estate agent to facilitate the sale or purchase of any plot, apartment or building, as the case may be, in real estate projects registered in the _____ State in terms of the Act and the rules and regulations made thereunder,

2. This registration is granted subject to the following conditions, namely:-
    (i) The real estate agent shall not facilitate the sale or purchase of any plot, apartment or building, as the case may be, in a real estate project or part of it, being sold by the promoter which is required but not registered with the regulatory authority;
    (ii) The real estate agent shall maintain and preserve such books of account, records and documents as provided under rule 14;
    (iii) The real estate agent shall not involve himself in any unfair trade practices as specified under clause (c) of section 10;
    (iv) The real estate agent shall provide assistance to enable the allottee and promoter to exercise their respective rights and fulfil their respective obligations at the time of booking and sale of any plot, apartment or building, as the case may be.
    (v) The real estate agent shall comply with the provisions of the Act and the rules and regulations made thereunder;
    (vi) The real estate agent shall not contravene the provisions of any other law for the time being in force in the area where the project is being developed;
    (vii) The real estate agent shall discharge such other functions as may be specified by the regulatory authority by regulations;

3. The registration is valid for a period of five years commencing from ……………… and ending with ……………… unless renewed by the regulatory authority in accordance with the provisions of the Act or the rules and regulations made thereunder.

4. If the above mentioned conditions are not fulfilled by the real estate agent, the regulatory authority may take necessary action against the real estate agent including revoking the registration granted herein, in accordance with the Act and the rules and regulations made thereunder.

Dated:
Place:

Signature and seal of the Authorized Officer
Real Estate Regulatory Authority

FORM 'I'
[See rule 11(2), 12(4), 13]

INTIMATION OF REJECTION OF APPLICATION FOR REGISTRATION OF REAL ESTATE AGENT / REJECTION OF APPLICATION FOR RENEWAL OF REGISTRATION OF REAL ESTATE AGENT / REVOCATION OF REGISTRATION OF REAL ESTATE AGENT

From:

    The Real Estate Regulatory Authority,

    …………………………………..

    …………………………………..

To

    …………………………………..

    …………………………………..

    …………………………………..

    Application / Registration No.: ………………………………….

    Dated: ………………………………….

You are hereby informed that your application for registration as real estate agent is rejected.

OR

You are hereby informed that your application for the renewal of the registration as real estate agent is rejected.

OR

You are hereby informed that the registration granted to you as real estate agent is hereby revoked.

for the reasons set out:- _…………………………………………………………………….

Place:
Dated:

Signature and seal of the Authorized Officer
Real Estate Regulatory Authority

FORM 'J'
[See rule 12(1)]

APPLICATION FOR RENEWAL OF REGISTRATION OF REAL ESTATE AGENT

From:

……………………………..

……………………………..

……………………………..

To

The Real Estate Regulatory Authority,

……………………………..

……………………………..

……………………………..

Sir,

I/we beg to apply for renewal my/our registration as a real estate agent under registration certificate bearing No. ………………….., which expires on ………………….

As required I/we submit the following documents and information, namely:-

(i) A demand draft no. ……………….. _dated ……………… for rupees ……………………………….. in favour of ……………………. drawn on ………………………………. bank as renewal fee;
(ii) The original registration certificate; and
(iii) Status of the applicant, whether individual / company / proprietorship firm / societies / partnership firm / limited liability partnership;
(iv) In case of individual –
    (a) Name
    (b) Father's Name
    (c) Occupation
    (d) Permanent address
    (e) Photograph

OR

In case of firm / societies / companies –
    (a) Name
    (b) Address
    (c) Copy of registration certificate
    (d) Major activities
    (e) Name, photograph and address of partners / directors

(v)　　income tax returns filed under the provisions of the Income Tax Act, 1961 for three financial years preceding the application or in case the applicant was exempted from filing returns under the provisions of the Income Tax Act, 1961 for any of the three year preceding the application, a declaration to such effect;
(vi)　　particulars of registration including the bye-laws, memorandum of association, articles of association etc. as the case may be;
(vii)　　authenticated copy of the address proof of the place of business;
(viii)　　Details of registration in any other State or Union territory;
(ix)　　Any other information as specified by regulations.

Dated:
Place:

Yours faithfully,
Signature and seal of the applicant(s)

FORM 'K'
[See rule 12(4)]

RENEWAL OF REGISTRATION OF REAL ESTATE AGENT

1. This renewal of registration is granted under section 9 of the Act to -

   (in the case of an individual) Mr./Ms. ………………………………… son of Mr./Ms. …………………………Tehsil …………… District ……………….. State …………………;

   OR

   (in the case of a firm / society / company) ………………………….. firm / society / company ……………………….. having its registered office/principal place of business at ……………………

   In continuation to registration certificate bearing No. ……………….., of ……………..

2. This renewal of registration is granted subject to the following conditions, namely:-

   (i) The real estate agent shall not facilitate the sale or purchase of any plot, apartment or building, as the case may be, in a real estate project or part of it, being sold by the promoter which is required but not registered with the regulatory authority;

   (ii) The real estate agent shall maintain and preserve such books of account, records and documents as provided under rule 14;

   (iii) The real estate agent shall not involve himself in any unfair trade practices as specified under clause (c) of section 10;

   (iv) The real estate agent shall facilitate the possession of all documents, as the allottee is entitled to, at the time of booking of any plot, apartment or building, as the case may be;

   (v) The real estate agent shall provide assistance to enable the allottee and promoter to exercise their respective rights and fulfil their respective obligations at the time of booking and sale of any plot, apartment or building, as the case may be;

   (vi) The real estate agent shall comply with the provisions of the Act and the rules and regulations made thereunder;

   (vii) The real estate agent shall not contravene the provisions of any other law for the time being in force in the area where the project is being developed;

   (viii) The real estate agent shall discharge such other functions as may be specified by the regulatory authority by regulations;

3. The registration is valid for a period of five years commencing from ………………………….. and ending with ……………………….. unless renewed by the regulatory authority in accordance with the provisions of the Act or the rules and regulations made thereunder.

4. If the above mentioned conditions are not fulfilled by the real estate agent, the regulatory authority may take necessary action against the real estate agent including revoking the registration granted herein, as per the Act and the rules and regulations made thereunder.

Dated:
Place:

Signature and seal of the Authorized Officer
Real Estate Regulatory Authority

By order and the name of the Governor of Gujarat,

(Neela Munshi)
Officer on Special Duty & Ex-Officio Joint Secretary
to the Government of Gujarat
Urban Development and Urban Housing Department

NOTIFICATION
Urban Development and Urban Housing Department
Sachivalaya, Gandhinagar.
Dated, the 29th October, 2016.

Real Estate (Regulation and Development) Act, 2016. No.GH/V/197 of 2016/MIS-102016-328145-L:- In exercise of the powers conferred by section 84 of the Real Estate (Regulation and Development) Act, 2016 (16 of 2016), the Government of Gujarat, hereby makes the following rules, namely: —

1. **Short title and Commencement.-**

    (1) These rules may be called the 'Gujarat Real Estate (Regulation and Development) (Matters Relating to the Gujarat Real Estate Appellate Tribunal) Rules, 2016.
    (2) It shall come into force with effect from the date of this notification.

2. **Definitions.-**

    (1) In these rules, unless the context otherwise requires, -

    (a) "Act" means the Real Estate (Regulation and Development) Act, 2016 (16 of 2016);
    (b) "Annexure" means an annexure appended to these rules;
    (c) "authenticated copy" shall mean a self-attested copy of any document required to be provided by any person under these rules;
    (d) "Authority" means the Real Estate Regulatory Authority as defined in clause (i) of section (2) of the Act;
    (d) "Form" means a form appended to these rules;
    (e) "Government" means the Government of Gujarat;
    (f) "section" means a section of the Act; and
    (g) "Appellate Tribunal" means the Gujarat Real Estate Appellate Tribunal established under section 43 of the Act.

    (2) Words and expressions used herein and not defined, but defined in the Act, shall have the meaning respectively assigned to them in the Act.

3. **Form for filing Appeal and the fees payable.-**

    (1) Every appeal filed under sub-section (1) of section 44 shall be accompanied by a fee of rupees one thousand in the form of a demand draft drawn on a nationalized bank in favour of the Appellate Tribunal and payable at the main branch of that Bank at the station where the seat of the said Appellate Tribunal is situated.

    (2) Every appeal shall be filed in Form 'A' along with the following documents:
    (a) An attested true copy of the order against which the appeal is filed;
    (b) Copies of the documents relied upon by the appellant and referred to in the appeal;
    (c) An index of the documents.

(3) Procedure for filing the appeal shall be as may be decided by the Appellate Tribunal.

4. **Manner of selection of members of the Appellate Tribunal.-**
    (1) As and when vacancy of a Member in the Appellate Tribunal exists or arises, or is likely to arise, the Government may make a reference to the Selection Committee in respect of the vacancy to be filled.

    (2) The Selection Committee may, for the purpose of selection of the Member of the Appellate Tribunal, follow such procedure as deemed fit including the appointment of a Search Committee consisting of such persons as the Selection Committee considers appropriate to suggest a panel of names possessing the requisite qualifications and experience and suitable for being considered for appointment as Member of the Appellate Tribunal.

    (3) The Selection Committee shall select two persons for each vacancy and recommend the same to the Government.

    (4) The Selection Committee shall make its recommendation to the Government within a period of sixty days from the date of reference made under sub-rule (1).

    (5) The Government shall within thirty days from the date of the recommendation by the Selection Committee, appoint one of the two persons recommended by the Selection Committee for the vacancy of the Member.

5. **Salary and allowances payable and other terms and conditions of service of Chairperson and Members of the Appellate Tribunal.-**
    (1) The salaries and allowances payable to the Chairperson and Members of the Appellate Tribunal shall be as follows:
        (a) The Chairperson shall be paid a monthly salary equivalent to the last drawn salary by such person, as a Judge of a High Court.
        (b) The Member shall be paid a monthly salary equivalent to the last drawn salary at the post held by such person, prior to his appointment as a Member of the Appellate Tribunal.
        (c) Every Member, who is not a servant of the Government, shall be paid a monthly salary equivalent to the Secretary to the Government.

    (2) The Chairperson and Members shall be entitled to thirty days of earned leave for every year of service.

    (3) The other allowances and conditions of service of the Chairperson and the Members shall be such as may be notified by the Government from time to time.

6. **Procedure for inquiry of the charges against the Chairperson or Member of the Authority or the Appellate Tribunal.-**
    (1) In the event of the Government becoming aware of occurrence of any of the

circumstances specified in clause (d) or clause (e) of sub-section (1) of section 26 in case of a Chairperson or Member of the Authority or as specified under sub-section (1) of section 49 in case of a Chairperson or Member of the Appellate Tribunal, by receipt of a complaint in this regard or *suo motu,* as the case may be, the Government shall make a preliminary scrutiny with respect to such charges against the Chairperson or any Member of the regulatory Authority or Appellate Tribunal, as the case may be.

(2) If, on preliminary scrutiny, the Government considers it necessary to investigate into the allegation, it shall place the complaint, if any, together with supporting material as may be available, before a Judge of the High Court.

(3) The Government shall forward to the Judge, copies of-
 (a) the statement of charges against the Chairperson or Member of the Authority or Appellate Tribunal, as the case may be; and
 (b) material documents relevant to the inquiry.

(4) The Chairperson or Member of the Authority or Appellate Tribunal, as the case may be, shall be given a reasonable opportunity of being heard with respect to the charges within the time period as may be specified in this behalf by the Judge.

(5) Where it is alleged that the Chairperson or Member of the Appellate Tribunal is unable to discharge the duties of his office efficiently due to any physical or mental incapacity and the allegation is denied, the Judge may arrange for the medical examination of the Chairperson or Member of the Appellate Tribunal.

(6) After the conclusion of the investigation, the Judge shall submit his report to the Government stating therein his findings and the reasons thereof on each of the articles of charges separately with such observations on the whole case as he thinks fit.

(7) The Government, thereafter shall in consultation with the Chief Justice of the High Court decide to either remove or not to remove the Chairperson or Member of the Authority or Appellate Tribunal, as the case may be.

7. **Salary and allowances payable and other terms and conditions of service of the officers and other employees of the Appellate Tribunal.-**
 (1) The conditions of service of the officers and employees of the Appellate Tribunal and any other category of employees in the matter of pay, allowances, leave, joining time, joining time pay, age of superannuation and other conditions of service, shall be regulated in accordance with such rules and regulations as are, from time to time, applicable to officers and employees of the Government drawing the corresponding scales of pay;

 (2) The Government shall have power to relax the provisions of any of these rules in respect of any class or category of officers or employees or consultants and experts, as the case may be.

8. **Additional powers of the Appellate Tribunal.-** The Appellate Tribunal may call upon such experts or consultants from the fields of economics, commerce, accountancy, real estate, competition, construction, architecture or engineering or from any other discipline as it deems necessary, to assist the Appellate Tribunal in the conduct of any inquiry or proceedings before it.

9. **Administrative powers of the Chairperson of the Appellate Tribunal.-** The administrative powers of the Chairperson of the Appellate Tribunal shall include making decisions with regard to the following:
   (a) matters pertaining to staff strength, wages and salaries structures, emoluments, perquisites and personnel policies;
   (b) matters pertaining to creation and abolition of posts;
   (c) matter pertaining to appointments, promotions and confirmation for all posts;
   (d) acceptance of resignations by any Member, officer or employee;
   (e) officiating against sanctioned posts;
   (f) authorization of tours to be undertaken by any Member, officer or employee: within and outside India and allowance to be granted for the same; (g) matters in relation to reimbursement of medical claims;
   (h) matters in relation to grant or rejection of leaves;
   (i) permission for hiring of vehicles for official use;
   (j) nominations for attending seminars, conferences and training courses in India or abroad;
   (k) permission for invitation of guests to carry out training course; (l) matters pertaining to staff welfare expenses;
   (m) sanction scrapping or write-off of capital assets which due to normal wear and tear have become unserviceable or are considered beyond economical repairs;
   (n) matters relating to disciplinary action against any Member, officer or employee;
   (o) any other powers that may be required for the efficient functioning of the Appellate Tribunal and enforcement of the provisions of the Act and these rules.

FORM 'A'
[See rule 3(2)]

APPEAL TO THE APPELLATE TRIBUNAL

Appeal under section 44 of the Act

Every appeal shall be filed in English and in case it is in some other Indian language, it shall be accompanied by a copy translated in English and shall be fairly and legibly type-written, lithographed or printed in double spacing on one side of standard petition paper with an inner margin of about four centimetres width on top and with a right margin on 2.5 cm, and left margin of 5 cm, duly paginated, indexed and stitched together in paper book form.

For use of Appellate Tribunal's office: Date of filing:

Date of receipt by post: _____

Registration No.: _____

Signature: _____

Registrar: _____

IN THE GUJARAT REAL ESTATE APPELLATE TRIBUNAL (Name of place)

Between

_____ Appellant(s)

And

_____ Respondent(s) Details of appeal:

1. Particulars of the appellants: (i) Name of the appellant:
   (ii) Address of the existing office / residence of the appellant: (iii) Address for service of all notices:

2. Particulars of the respondents: (i) Name(s) of respondent:
   (ii) Office address of the respondent: (iii) Address for service of all notices:

3. Jurisdiction of the Appellate Tribunal:
   The appellant declares that the subject matter of the appeal falls within the jurisdiction of the Appellate Tribunal.

4. Limitation:
   The appellant declares that the appeal is within the limitation specified in sub-section (2) of section 44
   OR
   If the appeal is filed after the expiry of the limitation period specified under sub-section (2) of section 44 specify reasons for delay_____

5. Facts of the case:
   (give a concise statement of facts and grounds of appeal against the specific order of Regulatory Authority or the Adjudicating Officer, as the case may be, passed under section(s) _____ of the Act.

6. Relief(s) sought:
   In view of the facts mentioned in paragraph 5 above, the appellant prays for the following relief(s) _____
   [Specify below the relief(s) sought explaining the grounds of relief(s) and the legal

provisions (if any) relied upon]

7. Interim order, if prayed for:
Pending final decision on the appeal the appellant seeks issue of the following interim order:

[Give here the nature of the interim order prayed for with reasons]

8. Matter not pending with any other court, etc.:
The appellant further declares that the matter regarding which this appeal has been made is not pending before any court of law or any other Authority or any other tribunal(s).

9. Particulars of bank draft in respect of the fee in terms of sub-rule (1) of rule 28:
    (i) Amount
    (ii) Name of the bank on which drawn
    (iii) Demand draft number

10. List of enclosures:
    (i) An attested true copy of the order against which the appeal is filed
    (ii) Copies of the documents relied upon by the appellant and referred to in the appeal
    (iii) An index of the documents

Verification

I_____ (name in full block letters) son / daughter of _____ the appellant do hereby verify that the contents of paragraphs [1 to 10] are true to my personal knowledge and belief and that I have not suppressed any material fact(s).

Place:
Date: Signature of the appellant(s)

By order and in the name of the Governor of Gujarat,

(Neela Munshi)
Officer on Special Duty & Ex-Officio Joint Secretary
to the Government of Gujarat
Urban Development and Urban Housing Department.

Copy forwarded with compliments to:
- Principal Secretary to Hon'ble Governor of Gujarat, Raj Bhavan, Gandhinagar. (By Letter)
- Principal Secretary to Hon'ble Chief Minister, Swarnim Sankul-1, Sachivalaya, Gandhinagar.
- Personal Secretary to Hon'ble Deputy Chief Minister, Swarnim Sankul-1, Sachivalaya, Gandhinagar.
- Personal Secretary to Hon'ble Minister of State for Urban Development, Swarnim Sankul-2, Sachivalaya, Gandhinagar.
- Municipal Commissioner, All Municipal Corporations.

- ❖ Chief Executive Authority, All Urban/Area Development Authorities.
- ❖ Director of Municipalities, Gujarat State, Gandhinagar – for Circulate all the Municipalities.
- ❖ Chief Officer, All Municipalities.
- ❖ Chief Town Planner, Gujarat State, Gandhinagar.
- ❖ Collector, All Districts.
- ❖ Senior Town Planner, All Region Office of Town Planning and Valuation Department.
- ❖ District Development Officer, All District Offices.
- ❖ Manager, Government Central Press, Gandhinagar – With a request to publish the aforesaid notification in Part-IV-B central section, in the Gujarat Government Extra Ordinary Gazette of **Dated 29/10/2016** and forward 10 printed copies of the same to this department. The Gujarati version of the Notification will be forwarded shortly to you by the Legislative and Parliamentary Affairs Department, Sachivalaya, Gandhinagar.
- ❖ Legislative and Parliamentary Affairs Department, Sachivalaya, Gandhinagar – With request to send Gujarati version of the said Notification directly to the Manger, Government Central Press, Gandhinagar for its publication in the official gazette urgently.
- ❖ Director of Information, Gandhinagar-with request to issue suitable presses note.
- ❖ The Revenue Department, New Sachivalaya, Gandhinagar.
- ❖ System Manager, Urban Development and Urban Housing Department, New Sachivalaya, Gandhinagar.
- ❖ The Select file of 'L' Branch, U.D. & U.H.Deptt.
- ❖ The personal file of Dy. Section Officer, L-Branch, U.D. & U.H.Deptt.

NOTIFICATION

Urban Development and Urban Housing Department
Sachivalaya, Gandhinagar
Dated, the 29th October, 2016.

Real Estate (Regulation and Development) Act, 2016. No.GH/V/196 of 2016/MIS-102016-328145-L:- In exercise of the powers conferred by section 84 of the Real Estate (Regulation and Development) Act, 2016 (16 of 2016), the Government of Gujarat hereby makes the following rules, namely: —

1. **Short title and Commencement.-**

   (1) These rules may be called the 'Gujarat Real Estate (Regulation and Development) (Matters Relating to the Real Estate Regulatory Authority) Rules, 2016.
   (2) It shall come into force with effect from the date of this notification.

2. **Definitions.-**

   (1) In these rules, unless the context otherwise requires, -

   (a) "Act" means the Real Estate (Regulation and Development) Act, 2016 (16 of 2016) ;
   (b) "authenticated copy" shall mean a self-attested copy of any document required to be provided by any person under these rules;
   (c) "Authority" means the Gujarat Real Estate Regulatory Authority as established under sub-section (1) of section 20 of the Act;
   (d) "Form" means a form appended to these rules;
   (e) "Government" means the Government of Gujarat;
   (f) "layout plan" means a plan of the project depicting the division or proposed division of land into plots, roads, open spaces, amenities, etc. and other details as may be necessary;
   (h) "section" means a section of the Act; and
   (i) "Selection Committee" means the Selection Committee as referred to in section 22 of the Act.

   (2) Words and expressions used herein and not defined, but defined in the Act, shall have the meaning respectively assigned to them in the Act.

3. **Manner of selection of Chairperson and Members of the Authority.-** (1) As and when the vacancy of a Chairperson or a Member in the Authority exists or arises, or is likely to arise, the Government may make a reference to the Selection Committee in respect of the vacancy to be filled.

   (2) The Selection Committee may, for the purpose of selection of the Chairperson or a Member of the Authority, follow such procedure as deemed fit including the appointment of a search committee consisting of such persons as the Selection Committee considers appropriate to suggest a panel of names possessing the requisite qualifications and experience and suitable for being considered for appointment as Chairperson or Member of the Authority.

   (3) The Selection Committee shall select two persons for each vacancy and recommend the same to the Government.

   (4) The Selection Committee shall make its recommendation to the Government within a period of sixty days from the date of reference made under sub- rule (1).

(5) The Government shall within thirty days from the date of the recommendation of the Selection Committee, appoint one of the two persons recommended by the Selection Committee for the vacancy of the Chairperson or the Member, as the case may be.

4. **Salary and allowances payable and other terms and conditions of service of Chairperson and Members of the Authority.-** (1) The salaries and allowances payable to the Chairperson and Members of the Authority shall be as follows, namely:-
   (a) The Chairperson shall be paid a consolidated monthly salary of two lakh fifty thousand rupees and he shall not be entitled to any allowance relating to house and vehicle.
   (b) The whole-time Member shall be paid a consolidated monthly salary of two lakh rupees and he shall not be entitled to any allowance relating to house and vehicle;
   (c) Every part-time member, who is not an employee of the Government, shall be paid a sitting fee for each day he attends the meetings of the Authority as may be determined by the Government, from time to time and he shall not be entitled to any allowance relating to house and vehicle.

   (2) The Chairperson and whole time Members shall be entitled to thirty days of earned leave for every year of service.

   (3) The other allowances and conditions of service of the Chairperson and the whole-time Member shall be such as may be notified by the Government.

5. **Administrative powers of the Chairperson of the regulatory Authority.-** The administrative powers of the Chairperson of the Authority shall include making decisions with regard to the following:
   (a) matters pertaining to staff strength and their wages and salary structures, emoluments, perquisites and personnel policies;
   (b) matters pertaining to creation and abolition of posts;
   (c) matter pertaining to appointments, promotions and confirmation for all posts;
   (d) acceptance of resignations by any Member, officer or employee;
   (e) officiating against sanctioned posts;
   (f) authorisation of tours to be undertaken by any Member, officer or employee within and outside India and allowances to be granted for the same;
   (g) matters in relation to reimbursement of medical claims;
   (h) matters in relation to grant or rejection of leaves;
   (i) permission for hiring of vehicles for official use;
   (j) nominations for attending seminars, conferences and training courses in India or abroad ;
   (k) permission for invitation of guests to carry out training course;
   (l) matters pertaining to staff welfare expenses;
   (m) sanction scrapping or writing-off of capital assets which due to normal wear and tear have become unserviceable or are considered beyond economical repairs;
   (n) matters relating to disciplinary action against any Member, officer or employee;
   (o) any other powers that may be required for the efficient functioning of the Authority and enforcement of the provisions of the Act and these rules.

6. **Salary and allowances payable and other terms and conditions of service of the officers and other employees of the Authority and experts and consultants engaged by the Authority.-** (1) The conditions of service of the officers and employees of the Authority and any other category of employees in the matter of pay, allowances, leave,

joining time, joining time pay, age of superannuation and other conditions of service, shall be regulated in accordance with such rules and regulations as are, from time to time, applicable to officers and employees of the Government drawing the corresponding scales of pay.

(2) The consultants or experts that may be engaged by the Authority-
- (a) shall be paid a monthly honorarium as may be determined by the Government from time to time;
- (b) shall not be deemed to be regular members of the staff borne on the establishment of the Authority;
- (c) may be appointed for a tenure of one year, extendable on year to year basis;
- (d) may be terminated by the Authority by serving one month's notice.

(3) The Government shall have power to relax the provisions of any of these rules in respect of any class or category of officers or employees or consultants and experts, as the case may be.

7. **Functioning of the Authority.-** (1) The office of the Authority shall be located at such place as may be determined by the Government by notification.

(2) The working days and office hours of the Authority shall be the same as that of the Government.

(3) The official common seal and emblem of the Authority shall be such as the Government may specify.

8. **Additional powers of the Authority.-** (1) In addition to the powers specified in sub-section (2) of section 35, the Authority shall have the following additional powers:

- (a) to require the promoter, allottee or real estate agent to furnish in writing such information or explanation or produce such documents within such reasonable time, as it may deem necessary;

- (b) to requisite, subject to the provisions of sections 123 and 124 of the Indian Evidence Act, 1872 (1 of 1872), any public record or document or copy of such record or document from any office.

(2) The Authority may call upon such experts or consultants from the fields of economics, commerce, accountancy, real estate, competition, construction, architecture or engineering or from any other discipline as it deems necessary, to assist the Authority in the conduct of any inquiry or proceedings before it.

(3) The Authority may in the interest of the allottees, enquire into the payment of amounts imposed as penalty, interest or compensation, paid or payable by the promoter, in order to ensure that the promoter has not-
- (a) withdrawn the said amounts from the account maintained as provided under sub-clause (l) of clause (l) of sub-section (2) of section 4; or
- (b) used any amounts paid to such promoter by the allottees for the that real estate project for which the penalty, interest or compensation is payable, or any other real estate project;
- (c) recovered the amounts paid as penalty, fine or compensation from the allottees of the relevant real estate project or any other real estate project.

9. **Manner of recovery of interest, penalty and compensation.-** Subject to the provisions of sub-section (1) of section 40, the recovery of the amounts due as arrears of land revenue shall be carried out in the manner provided in the Gujarat Land Revenue Code, 1879.

Bom. V of 1879

10. **Details to be published on the website.-** (1) For the purpose of clause (b) of section 34, the Authority shall ensure that the following information shall be made available on its website in respect of each project registered-

    (a) Details of the promoter including the following:

       (i) Developer or Group Profile:
           (A) a brief detail of his enterprise including its name, registered address, type of enterprise (proprietorship, limited liability partnership, society, partnership, company, competent Authority) and the particulars of registration and in case of a newly incorporated or registered entity, brief details of the of the parent entity including its name, registered address, type of enterprise (proprietorship, societies, limited liability partnership, partnership, companies, competent Authority);
           (B) background of promoter- educational qualification, work experience and in case of a newly incorporated or registered entity work experience of the parent entity.
           (C) name, address, contact details and photograph of the promoter in case of an individual and the name, address, contact details and photograph of the chairman, directors, partners, as the case may be and that of the authorised persons.

       (ii) Track record of the promoter:
           (A) number of years of experience of the promoter or parent entity in real estate construction in the state/union territory;
           (B) number of years of experience of the promoter or parent entity in real estate construction in other states or union territories;
           (C) number of completed projects and area constructed till date;
           (D) number of ongoing projects and proposed area to be constructed;
           (E) details and profile of ongoing and completed projects for the last 5 years as provided under clause (b) of sub-section (2) of section 4.

       (iii) Litigations: Details of litigations in the past five years in relation to the real estate projects developed or being developed by the promoter.

       (iv) Website:
           (A) web link to the developer or group website;
           (B) web link to the project website.

    (b) Details of the real estate project including the following:

    (i) compliance and registration:
           (A) authenticated copy of the approvals and commencement certificate from the competent Authority as provided under clause (c) of sub-section (2) of section 4;
           (B) the sanctioned plan, layout plan and specifications of the project or the phase thereof, and the whole project as sanctioned by the competent Authority as provided under clause (d) of sub-section (2) of section 4;
           (C) details of the registration granted by the Authority.

(ii) Apartment and garage related details:
   (A) details of the number, type and carpet area of apartments for sale in the project as provided under clause (h) of sub-section (2) of section 4;
   (B) details of the number and areas of garage for sale in the project as provided under clause (i) of sub-section (2) of section 4;
   (C) details of the number of open parking areas available in the real estate project.

(iii) Registered Agents: Names and addresses of real estate agents as provided under clause (j) of sub-section (2) of section 4.

(iv) Consultants: Details, including name and addresses of contractors, architect and structural engineers and other persons concerned with the development of the real estate project as provided under clause (k) of sub-section (2) of section 4, such as:-
   (A) name and address of the firm
   (B) names of promoters
   (C) year of establishment
   (D) names and profile of key projects completed

(v) Location: the location details of the project, with clear demarcation of land dedicated for the project along with its boundaries including the latitude and longitude of the end points of the project as provided under clause (f) of sub-section (2) of section 4.

(vi) Development Plan:
   (A) The plan of development works to be executed in the proposed project and the proposed facilities to be provided thereof including fire fighting facilities, drinking water facilities, emergency evacuation services, use of renewable energy etc. as provided under clause (e) of sub-section (2) of section 4;
   (B) Amenities: a detailed note explaining the salient features of the proposed project including access to the project, design for electric supply including street lighting, water supply arrangements and site for disposal and treatment of storm and sullage water, any other facilities and amenities or public health services proposed to be provided in the project;
   (C) Gantt Charts and Project schedule: the plan of development works to be executed in the project and the details of the proposed facilities to be provided thereof.

(c) Financials of the promoter:

  (i)   authenticated copy of the PAN card of the promoter

  (ii) the annual report including audited profit and loss account, balance sheet, cash flow statement, directors report and the auditors report of the promoter for the immediately preceding three financial years and where annual report is not available then the audited profit and lost account, balance sheet, cash flow statement and the auditors report of the promoter for the immediately preceding three financial years and in case of newly incorporated or registered entity such information shall be disclosed for the parent entity;

(d) The promoter shall upload the following updates on the webpage for the project, within seven days from the expiry of each quarter:
   (i) List of number and types of apartments or plots, as the case may be booked; (ii)

   List of number of garages booked;

   (iii) Status of the project:
      (A) Status of construction of each building with photographs;
      (B) Status of construction of each floor with photographs;
      (C) Status of construction of internal infrastructure and common areas with photographs.

   (iv) Status of approvals:
      (A) Approval received;
      (B) Approvals applied and expected date of receipt;
      (C) Approvals to be applied and date planned for application;
      (D) Modifications, amendment or revisions, if any, issued by the competent Authority with regard to any license, permit or approval for the project.

(e) Downloads:
   (i) Approvals:
      (A) No Objection certificates
         – Consent to Establish and Operate;
         – Environmental Clearance;
         – Fire NOC;
         – Height clearance from Airport Authority of India;
         – Such other approvals as may be required and obtained for the project.
      (B) Authenticated copy of the license or land use permission, building sanction plan and the commencement certificate from the competent Authority obtained in accordance with the laws applicable for the project, and where the project is proposed to be developed in phases, an authenticated copy of the license or land use permission, building sanction plan and the commencement certificate for each of such phases;
      (C) Authenticated copy of the site plan or site map showing the location of the project land along with names of revenue estates, survey numbers, cadastral numbers, khasra numbers and area of each parcels of the project land;
      (D) Authenticated copy of the layout plan of the project or the phase thereof, and also the layout plan of the whole project as sanctioned by the competent Authority;
      (E) Floor plans for each tower and block including clubhouse, amenities and common areas;
      (F) Any other permission, approval, or licence that may be required under applicable law;
      (G) Authenticated copy of occupancy certificate and completion certificate including its application.

   (ii) Legal Documents:
      (A) Details including the proforma of the application form, allotment letter, agreement for sale and the conveyance deed;
      (B) Authenticated copy of the legal title deed reflecting the title of the promoter to the land on which development is proposed to be developed along with legally valid documents with authentication of such title, if such land is owned by another person;

(C) Land Title Search Report from an advocate having experience of at least ten years in land related matters;

(D) Details of encumbrances on the land on which development is proposed including any rights, title, interest or name of any party in or over such land along with details or no encumbrance certificate from an advocate having experience of at-least ten years in land related matters;

(E) where the promoter is not the owner of the land on which development is proposed details of the consent of the owner of the land along with a copy of the collaboration agreement, development agreement, joint development agreement or any other agreement, as the case may be, entered into between the promoter and such owner and copies of title and other documents reflecting the title of such owner on the land proposed to be developed;

(F) Sanction letters:
   – From banks for construction finance;
   – From banks for home loan tie-ups.

(f) Contact details: Contact address, contact numbers and email-ids of the promoter and other officials handling the project.

(g) Such other documents or information as may be specified by the Act or the rules and regulations made thereunder.

(2) For the purpose of clause (c) of section 34, the regulatory Authority shall maintain a database and ensure that the information specified therein shall be made available on its website in respect of each project revoked or penalised, as the case may be.

(3) For the purpose of clause (d) of section 34, the regulatory Authority shall ensure that the following information shall be made available on its website in respect of each real estate agent registered with it or whose application for registration has been rejected or revoked.

(a) For real estate agents registered with the Authority:

   (i) registration number and the period of validity of the registration of the real estate agent with the regulatory Authority;

   (ii) brief details of his enterprise including its name, registered address, type of enterprise (proprietorship, societies, partnership, companies etc.);

   (iii) particulars of registration including the bye-laws, memorandum of association, articles of association etc. as the case may be;

   (iv) photograph of the real estate agent if it is and individual and the photograph of the partners, directors etc. in case of other persons;

   (v) authenticated copy of the PAN card;

   (vi) authenticated copy of the address proof of the place of business and the contact address, contact numbers and email-ids of the real estate agent and other officials responsible.

(b) In case of applicants whose application for registration as a real estate agent have been rejected or real estate agents whose registration has been revoked by the regulatory Authority:

(i) registration number and the period of validity of the registration of the real estate agent with the regulatory Authority;

(ii) brief details of his enterprise including its name, registered address, type of enterprise (proprietorship, societies, partnership, companies etc.);

(iii) photograph of the real estate agent if it is and individual and the photograph of the partners, directors etc. in case of other persons.

(c) Such other documents or information as may be specified by the Act or the rules and regulations made thereunder.

(4) The Authority shall maintain a back-up, in digital form, of the contents of its website in terms of this rule, and ensure that such back-up is updated on the last day of each month.

11. **Manner of filing a complaint with the Authority and the manner of holding an inquiry by the Authority.-** (1) Any aggrieved person may file a complaint with the Authority for any violation under the Act or the rules and regulations made thereunder, save as those provided to be adjudicated by the adjudicating officer, as per Form 'A' which shall be accompanied by a fee of rupees one thousand in the form of a demand draft drawn on a nationalized bank in favour of regulatory Authority and payable at the main branch of that bank at the station where the seat of the said regulatory Authority is situated.

(2) The Authority shall for the purposes of deciding any complaint as specified under sub-rule (1), follow summary procedure for inquiry in the following manner:

(a) Upon receipt of the complaint the Authority shall issue a notice along with particulars of the alleged contravention and the relevant documents to the respondent;

(b) The notice shall specify a date and time for further hearing;

(c) On the date so fixed, the Authority shall explain to the respondent about the contravention alleged to have been committed in relation to any of the provisions of the Act or the rules and regulations made thereunder and if the respondent:

(i) pleads guilty, the regulatory Authority shall record the plea, and pass such orders including imposition of penalty as it thinks fit in accordance with the provisions of the Act or the rules and regulations, made thereunder;

(ii) does not plead guilty and contests the complaint the regulatory Authority shall demand and explanation from the respondent;

(d) Incase the Authority is satisfied on the basis of the submissions made that the complaint does not require any further inquiry it may dismiss the complaint;

(e) In case the Authority is satisfied on the basis of the submissions made that the there is need for further hearing into the complaint it may order production of documents or other evidence on a date and time fixed by it;

(f) The Authority shall have the power to carry out an inquiry into the complaint on the basis of documents and submissions;

(g) On the date so fixed, the Authority upon consideration of the evidence produced before it and other records and submissions is satisfied that -

(i) the respondent is in contravention of the provisions of the Act or the rules and regulations made thereunder it shall pass such orders including imposition of penalty as it thinks fit in accordance with the provisions of the Act or the rules and regulations made thereunder;

(ii) the respondent is not in contravention of the provisions of the Act or the rules and regulations made thereunder the Authority may, by order in writing, dismiss the complaint, with reasons to be recorded in writing.
(h) If any person fails, neglects or refuses to appear, or present himself as required before the Authority, the Authority shall have the power to proceed with the inquiry in the absence of such person or persons after recording the reasons for doing so.

12. **Manner of filing a complaint with the adjudicating officer and the manner of holding an inquiry by the adjudicating officer.-** (1) Any aggrieved person may file a complaint with the adjudicating officer for compensation under section 12, 14, 18 and 19 as per Form 'B' which shall be accompanied by a fee of rupees one thousand in the form of a demand draft drawn on a nationalized bank in favour of Authority and payable at the main branch of that bank at the station where the seat of the said Authority is situated.

(2) The adjudicating officer shall for the purposes of adjudging compensation follow summary procedure for inquiry in the following manner:
(i) Upon receipt of the complaint the adjudicating officer shall issue a notice along with particulars of the alleged contravention and the relevant documents to the promoter;
(j) The notice shall specify a date and time for further hearing;
(k) On the date so fixed, the adjudicating officer shall explain to the promoter about the contravention alleged to have been committed in relation to any of the provisions of the Act or the rules and regulations made thereunder and if the promoter:
(iii) pleads guilty, the adjudicating officer shall record the plea, and award such compensation as he thinks fit in accordance with the provisions of the Act or the rules and regulations, made thereunder;
(iv) does not plead guilty and contests the complaint the adjudicating officer shall demand and explanation from the promoter;
(l) In case the adjudicating officer is satisfied on the basis of the submissions made that the complaint does not require any further inquiry it may dismiss the complaint;
(m) In case the adjudicating officer is satisfied on the basis of the submissions made that the there is need for further hearing into the complaint it may order production of documents or other evidence on a date and time fixed by him;
(n) The adjudicating officer shall have the power to carry out an inquiry into the complaint on the basis of documents and submissions;
(o) On the date so fixed, the adjudicating officer upon consideration of the evidence produced before him and other records and submissions is satisfied that the promoter is-
(iii) liable to pay compensation, the adjudicating officer may, by order in writing, order payment of such compensation, as deemed fit by the promoter to the complainant; or
(iv) not liable to any compensation, the adjudicating officer may, by order in writing, dismiss the complaint, with reasons to be recorded in writing.
(p) If any person fails, neglects or refuses to appear, or present himself as required before the adjudicating officer, the adjudicating officer shall have the power to proceed with the inquiry in the absence of such person or persons after recording the reasons for doing so.

13. **Budget, accounts and audit.-** The Authority shall prepare a budget, maintain proper accounts and other relevant records and prepare an annual statement of accounts as provided in section 77 as per Form 'C'.

14. **Report and Returns.-** The Authority shall prepare its annual report as provided in section 78 as per Form 'D'.

FORM 'A'
[See rule 11(1)]

COMPLAINT TO REGULATORY AUTHORITY

Complaint under section 31 of the Act

For use of Regulatory Authority(s) office:

Date of filing: _____

Date of receipt by post: _____

Complaint No.: _____

Signature: _____

Registrar: _____

IN THE REGULATORY AUTHORITIES OFFICE (Name of place)

Between

_____ Complainant(s)

And

_____ Respondent(s)

Details of claim:

1. Particulars of the complainant(s):
   (i) Name of the complainant:
   (ii) Address of the existing office / residence of the complainant:
   (iii) Address for service of all notices:

2. Particulars of the respondents:
   (i) Name(s) of respondent:
   (ii) Office address of the respondent:
   (iii) Address for service of all notices:

3. Jurisdiction of the regulatory Authority:

   The complainant declares that the subject matter of the claim falls within the jurisdiction of the regulatory Authority.

4. Facts of the case:

   [give a concise statement of facts and grounds for complaint]

5. Relief(s) sought:

   In view of the facts mentioned in paragraph 4 above, the complainant prays for the following relief(s) _____

   [Specify below the relief(s) claimed explaining the grounds of relief(s) and the legal provisions (if any) relied upon]

6. Interim order, if prayed for:

   Pending final decision on the complaint the complainant seeks issue of the following interim order:

   [Give here the nature of the interim order prayed for with reasons]

7. Complainant not pending with any other court, etc.:

   The complainant further declares that the matter regarding which this complaint has been made is not pending before any court of law or any other Authority or any other tribunal(s).

8. Particulars of bank draft in respect of the fee in terms of sub-rule (1) of rule 36:
   (i) Amount
   (ii) Name of the bank on which drawn
   (iii) Demand draft number

9. List of enclosures:
   [Specify the details of enclosures with the complaint]

Verification

I_____ (name in full block letters) son / daughter of _____ the complainant do hereby verify that the contents of paragraphs [1 to 9] are true to my personal knowledge and belief and that I have not suppressed any material fact(s).

Place:
Date:

Signature of the complainant(s)

FORM 'B'
[See rule 12(1)]

APPLICATION TO ADJUDICATING OFFICER

Claim for compensation under section 31 read with section 71 of the Act

For use of Adjudicating Officers office:

Date of filing: _____

Date of receipt by post: _____

Application No.: _____

Signature: _____

Authorized Officer: _____

IN THE ADJUDICATING OFFICER'S OFFICE (Name of place)

Between

_____ applicant(s)

And

_____ Respondent(s)

Details of claim:

1. Particulars of the applicant(s):
   (i) Name of the applicant:
   (ii) Address of the existing office / residence of the appellant:
   (iii) Address for service of all notices:
   (iv) Details of allottees apartment, plot or building

2. Particulars of the respondents:
   (i) Name(s) of respondent:
   (ii) Office address of the respondent:
   (iii) Address for service of all notices:
   (iv) Registration no. and address of project:

3. Jurisdiction of the Adjudicating Officer:

   The applicant declares that the subject matter of the claim falls within the jurisdiction of the adjudicating officer.

4. Facts of the case:

   [give a concise statement of facts and grounds of claim against the promoter]

5. Compensation(s) sought:

In view of the facts mentioned in paragraph 4 above, the applicant prays for the following compensation(s) _____

[Specify below the compensation(s) claimed explaining the grounds of claim(s) and the legal provisions (if any) relied upon]

6. Claim not pending with any other court, etc.:

The applicant further declares that the matter regarding which this appeal has been made is not pending before any court of law or any other Authority or any other tribunal(s).

7. Particulars of bank draft in respect of the fee in terms of sub-rule (1) of rule 36:
   (iv) Amount
   (v) Name of the bank on which drawn
   (vi) Demand draft number

8. List of enclosures:
   [Specify the details of enclosures with the application]

Verification

I_____ (name in full block letters) son / daughter of _____ the applicant do hereby verify that the contents of paragraphs [1 to 8] are true to my personal knowledge and belief and that I have not suppressed any material fact(s).

Place:
Date:

Signature of the applicant(s)

FORM 'C'
[See rule 13]

ANNUAL STATEMENT OF ACCOUNTS

Receipts and Payments Account
For the year ended _____

(In Rupees)

A/c Code	Receipts	Current year As on	Previous Year As on	A/c Code	Payments	Current year As on	Previous year As on
1.	To Balance Brought down:			13.	By Chairperson and Members:		
1.1.	To Bank			13.1.	By Pay and Allowances		
1.2.	To Cash in hand			13.2.	By Other benefits		
2.	To Fee, Charges and Fine:			13.3.	By Travelling expenses:		
2.1.	To Fees			13.3.1.	By Overseas		
2.2.	To Charges			13.3.2.	By Domestic		
2.3.	To Fines			14.	By Officers:		
2.4.	To Others (specify)			14.1.	By Pay and Allowances		
3.	To Grants:			14.2.	By Retirement benefits		
3.1.	To Accounts with Government			14.3.	By Other benefits		
3.2.	To Others (specify)			14.4.	By Travelling expenses:		
4.	To Gifts			14.4.1.	By Overseas		
5.	To Seminars and conferences			14.4.2.	By Domestic		
6.	To Sale of Publications			15.	By Staff:		
7.	To Income on investments and Deposits :			15.1.	By Pay and Allowances		
7.1.	To Income on investments			15.2.	By Retirement benefits		
7.2.	To Income on Deposits			15.3.	By Other benefits		
8.	To Loans:			15.4.	By Travelling expenses:		
8.1.	To Government			15.4.1.	By Overseas		
8.2.	To Others (specify)			15.4.2.	By Domestic		

9.	To Sale of Assets			16.	By Hire of Conveyance		
10.	To Sale on Investments			17.	By Wages		
11.	To Recoveries from pay bills			18.	By Overtime		
				19.	By Honorarium		
				20.	By Other office expenses		
				21.	By Expenditure on Research		
				22.	By Consultation expenses		
				23.	By Seminars and conferences		
				24.	By Publications of Authority		
				25.	By Rent and Taxes		
				26.	By Interest on Loans		
				27.	By Promotional Expenses		
				28.	By Membership fee		
				29.	By Subscription		
				30.	By Purchase of Fixed Assets (specify)		
				31.	By Investments and Deposits:		
				31.1	By Investments		
				31.2	By Deposits		
				32.	By Security Deposits		
				33.	By Loans and Advances to:		
				33.1	By Employees:		
				33.1.1.	By Bearing Interest		
				33.1.2.	By Not bearing Interest		
				33.2.	By Suppliers/contractors		
				33.3.	By others (specify)		
				34.	By Repayment of loan		
				35.	By Others		
				35.1.	By Leave Salary and Pension		
				35.2.	Contribution		
				35.3.	By Audit Fee		
				35.4.	By Misc:		
				36.	By Balance carried down:		
				36.1	By Bank		

				36.2	By Cash in hand		
	Total				Total		

Member(s) (Signature)   Chairperson (Signature)

Income and Expenditure Account

For the 1st April _____ to 31st March _____

(In Rupees)

A/c Code	Expenditure	Current Year As on	Previous Year As on	A/c Code	Income	Current Year As on	Previous Year As on
37.	To Chairperson and Members			61.	By Fee, Charges and Fine		
37.1.	To Pay and Allowances			61.1.	By Fee		
37.2.	To Other benefits			61.2.	By Charges		
37.3.	To Travelling Expenses			61.3.	By Fines		
37.3.1.	To Overseas			61.4.	By Others (specify)		
37.3.2.	To Domestic			62.	By Grants		
38.	To Officers			62.1.	By Account with Government		
38.1.	To Pay and Allowances			62.2.	By Others (Specify)		
38.2.	To retirement Benefits			63.	By Gifts		
38.3.	To Other Benefits			64.	By Seminars and Conferences		
38.4.	To Traveling Expenses			65.	By Sale of Publications		
38.4.1.	To Overseas			66.	By Income on investments and Deposits		
38.4.2.	To Domestic			66.1.	By Income on investments		
39.	To Staff			66.2.	By Income on Deposits		
39.1.	To Pay and Allowances			66.3.	By Interest on Loan and Advances		
39.2.	To Retirement Benefits			67.	By Miscellaneous Income		
39.3.	To Other Benefits			67.1.	By Gain on Sales of Assets		
39.4.	To Traveling expenses			67.2.	By Excess of expenditure over		

					income		
39.4.1.	To Overseas			67.3.	(Transferred to Capital Fund Account)		
39.4.2.	To Domestic						
40.	To hire of Conveyance						
41.	To Wages						
42.	To Overtime						
43.	To Honorarium						
44.	To Other office expenses						
45.	To expenditure on Research						
46.	To Consultation expenses						
47.	To Seminars and conferences						
48.	To Publications of Real Estate Regulatory Authority						
49.	To Rent and Taxes						
50.	To Interest on loans						
51.	To Promotional Expenses						
52.	To membership fee						
53.	To Subscription						
54.	To Others						
54.1.	To Leave Salary and Pension						
54.2.	Contribution						
54.3.	To Audit Fee						
54.4.	To Misc.						
55.	To Depreciation						
56.	To Loss on sale of assets						
57.	To Bad Debts written off						
58.	To Provision for bad & doubtful debts						
59.	To Excess of income over Expenditure						
60.	(Transferred to capital Fund Account)						
	Total				Total		

Member(s) (Signature)   Chairperson (Signature)

Balance Sheet as on 31st March _____

(In Rupees)

A/c Code	Liabilities	Current Year As on	Previous Year As on	A/c Code	Assets	Current Year As on	Previous Year As on
68.	Funds			72.	Fixed Assets		
68.1.	Capital Fund			72.1.	Gross Block at Cost		
68.2.	Add Excess of Income over Expenditure/less excess of Expenditure over Income			72.2.	Less Cumulative depreciation		
68.3.	Other Funds (Specify)			72.3.	Net Block		
69.	Reserves			73.	Capital Work-in-progress		
70.	Loans			74.	Investments & Deposits		
70.1.	Government			74.1.	Investment		
70.2.	Others			74.2.	Deposits		
71.	Current Liabilities and provisions			75.	Loans and Advances		
				75.1.	Account with Government		
				76.	Sundry Debtors		
				77.	Cash and Bank Balances		
				78.	Other Current Assets		
	Total				Total		

Accounting Policies and Notes:

Member(s) (Signature)   Chairperson (Signature)

FORM 'D'
[See rule 14]

ANNUAL REPORT TO BE PREPARED BY THE AUTHORITY

I. Return on registration of promoters and real estate agents

A. In relation to Promoters:

Serial Number	Name of promoter	Address of promoter	Description of project for which registration has been issued	Fee paid	Registration Number
1	2	3	4	5	6

Date of issue of registration	Date on which registration expires	Date of extension of registration with period of extension	Remark
7	8	9	10

B. In relation to Real Estate Agents:

Serial Number	Name of Real Estate Agent	Address of Real Estate Agent	Registration Fee paid	Date of issue of registration certificate	Date on which registration certificate expires	Date and period of renewal of registration certificate	Remark
1	2	3	4	5	6	7	8

II. Return on number of cases filed before the regulatory Authority and the adjudicating officer for settlement of disputes and adjudicated upon.

Sl. No.	No. of Cases pending in the last quarter by the regulatory Authority	No. of Cases received during the quarter by the regulatory Authority	No. of Cases disposed of by the regulatory Authority

Sl. No.	No. of Cases pending in the last quarter with the adjudicating officer	No. of Cases received during the quarter by the adjudicating officer	No. of Cases disposed of by the adjudicating officer

III. Statement on the periodical survey conducted by the regulatory Authority to monitor the compliance of the provisions of the Act by the promoters, allottees and real estate agents.

Sl. No.	Survey conducted during the quarter with details	Observation of Authority	Remedial steps taken

IV. Statement on steps taken to mitigate any non-compliance of the provisions of the and the rules and regulations made thereunder by the promoters, allottees and real estate agents.

Sl. No.	Subject	Steps taken	Results achieved

V. Statements on penalty imposed by the regulatory Authority for contraventions of the Act and directions of the regulatory Authority and adjudicating officer.

Sl. No.	Name of the promoter	Details of the directions issued	Penalty imposed	Whether paid

Sl. No.	Name of the allottee	Details of the directions issued	Penalty imposed	Whether paid

Sl. No.	Name of the real estate agent	Details of the directions issued	Penalty imposed	Whether paid

By order and in the name of the Governor of Gujarat,

(Neela Munshi)
Officer on Special Duty & Ex-Officio Joint Secretary
to the Government of Gujarat
Urban Development and Urban Housing Department.

Copy forwarded with compliments to:
- Principal Secretary to Hon'ble Governor of Gujarat, Raj Bhavan, Gandhinagar. (By Letter)

- Principal Secretary to Hon'ble Chief Minister, Swarnim Sankul-1, Sachivalaya, Gandhinagar.
- Personal Secretary to Hon'ble Deputy Chief Minister, Swarnim Sankul-1, Sachivalaya, Gandhinagar.
- Personal Secretary to Hon'ble Minister of State for Urban Development, Swarnim Sankul-2, Sachivalaya, Gandhinagar.
- Municipal Commissioner, All Municipal Corporations.
- Chief Executive Authority, All Urban/Area Development Authorities.
- Director of Municipalities, Gujarat State, Gandhinagar – for Circulate all the Municipalities.
- Chief Officer, All Municipalities.
- Chief Town Planner, Gujarat State, Gandhinagar.
- Collector, All Districts.
- Senior Town Planner, All Region Office of Town Planning and Valuation Department.
- District Development Officer, All District Offices.
- Manager, Government Central Press, Gandhinagar – With a request to publish the aforesaid notification in Part-IV-B central section, in the Gujarat Government Extra Ordinary Gazette of **Dated 29/10/2016** and forward 10 printed copies of the same to this department. The Gujarati version of the Notification will be forwarded shortly to you by the Legislative and Parliamentary Affairs Department, Sachivalaya, Gandhinagar.
- Legislative and Parliamentary Affairs Department, Sachivalaya, Gandhinagar – With request to send Gujarati version of the said Notification directly to the Manger, Government Central Press, Gandhinagar for its publication in the official gazette urgently.
- Director of Information, Gandhinagar-with request to issue suitable presses note.
- The Revenue Department, New Sachivalaya, Gandhinagar.
- System Manager, Urban Development and Urban Housing Department, New Sachivalaya, Gandhinagar.
- The Select file of 'L' Branch, U.D. & U.H.Deptt.
- The personal file of Dy. Section Officer, L-Branch, U.D. & U.H.Deptt.

GUJARAT REAL ESTATE REGULATORY AUTHORITY
Gandhinagar
Dated the 7th September, 2017

GUJARAT REAL ESTATE REGULATORY AUTHORITY (GENERAL) REGULATIONS, 2017

No: Gujarat RERA.2017/General Regulations/1 In exercise of the powers conferred on it under sub-section (1) and clause (i) of sub-section (2) of section 85 of the Real Estate (Regulation and Development) Act, 2016 and of all other powers enabling it in that behalf, the Gujarat Real Estate Regulatory Authority hereby makes the following Regulations:-

Short Title and Commencement:

1. (a) These Regulations may be called the Gujarat Real Estate Regulatory Authority (General) Regulations 2017.
   (b) These Regulations shall come into force on the date of their notification in the Official Gazette.
   Definitions
2. (a) In these Regulations, unless the context otherwise requires:-

(i) "Act" means the Real Estate (Regulation and Development) Act 2016 as amended from time to time;

(ii) "Adjudication" means the process of arriving at decisions on complaints received by the Authority or the Adjudicating Officer under Section 31 of the Act;

(iii) "Chairperson" means the Chairperson of the Authority.

(iv) "Authority" means the Gujarat Real Estate Regulatory Authority;

(v) "Consultant" includes any person not in the employment of the Authority who may be appointed as such to assist the Authority on any matter required to be dealt with by the Authority under the Act and the rules and regulations made thereunder;

(vi) "Member" means a member of the Authority;

(vii) "Proceedings" means and include proceedings of all nature that the Authority may conduct in the discharge of its functions under the Act and the rules and regulations;

(viii) "Secretary" means the Secretary of the Authority ;

(ix) "Officer" means an officer of the Authority;

(x) "rule" means the rules made under the Act.

(xi) "Regulations" mean the Gujarat Real Estate Regulatory Authority (General) Regulations 2017 as amended from time to time.

(b) Words or expressions occurring in these Regulations and not defined herein but defined in the Act or the Rules shall bear the same meanings respectively assigned to them in the Act and the Rules.

Formats of Certificates of Architect, Engineer and Chartered Accountant:

3. The certificates to be issued by the project architect, project engineer, chartered accountant in practice for withdrawal of money from the separate account maintained under section 4(2) (l) (D) shall be in Form 1, 2 and 3 respectively. The certificate required to be issued by the Project Architect/Project Engineer on completion of each of the building/wing of the real estate project shall be in Form 4.

Additional Disclosures by Promoters on the Website and Project site:

4. In addition to all the details of the proposed Real Estate project, to be uploaded by the promoter on his webpage on the website of the Authority, as required under sub-section (1) of Section 11 of the Act and Rule 3 and 4 of the Gujarat Real Estate (Regulation and Development) (General) Rules 2017, the promoter shall upload the the annual report on statement of accounts, in Form 5 (issued in accordance with the third proviso to section 4(2) of the Act) duly certified and signed by the chartered accountant in practice who is the statutory auditor of the promoter's enterprise.

Explanation 1: The chartered accountant certifying the progress of the registered real estate project for the purpose of withdrawal of amounts from the separate account should be a "different entity" than the chartered accountant who is the statutory auditor of the promoter's enterprise.

Explanation 2: If the Form 5 issued by the statutory auditor reveals that any certificate issued by the project architect, engineer or the chartered accountant has false or incorrect information and the amounts collected for a particular project have not been utilized for the project and the withdrawal has not been in compliance with the proportion to the percentage of completion of the project, the Authority, in addition to taking penal actions as contemplated in the Act and the Rules, shall also take up the matter with the concerned regulatory body of the said professionals of the architect, engineer or chartered accountant, for necessary penal action against them, including cancellation of registration of membership for practice as such. Displaying of plans etc.,

5. The sanctioned plans, layout plans, along with specifications, approved by the Competent Authority shall be prominently displayed by the promoter at the project site.

Authority's Office, office hours and sittings:

6. The head office of the Authority shall be at Gandhinagar or such place as Government may decide to shift it to. The authority may, by order, establish benches and its offices at other places in the State.
7. The Authority shall follow the office timings and holidays as notified from time to time by the State Government for its offices in Gujarat and elsewhere, unless otherwise decided by the Authority.
8. The Authority may conduct its proceedings at the head office or at any other place within its jurisdiction on days and time as directed by the Chairperson.

Language of the Authority:

9. The proceedings of the Authority shall be conducted in English, provided that the Authority shall allow any person to plead or represent his case in Gujarati.
10. The Authority, at its sole discretion, may accept complaint petitions made in English or Gujarati, provided that if the Authority directs the same is to be accompanied by a translation thereof in English.

Provided that such translation may be dispensed with at the discretion of the Authority.

11. Any translation which is agreed to by the parties to the proceedings or which any of the parties furnish, may be accepted by the Authority as a true translation.
12. The Authority may, in appropriate cases, direct translation of Petitions and their accompanying documents into English or Gujarati.

Seal of the Authority:

13. Any document requiring authentication by the Authority shall be issued under the seal of the Authority, and shall be signed by the Secretary or other Officer authorized by the Chairperson in this behalf.

Officers of the Authority:

14. (a) The Authority shall have the power to appoint the Secretary, Officers and other employees for discharging various duties and perform certain functions. The qualifications, experience and terms and conditions of service and appointment of such Secretary, Officers and other employees shall be subject to such regulations as may be specified by the Authority.

    (b) The Authority may appoint, engage or retain Consultants, Lawyers, Experts to assist the Authority in the

    discharge of its functions.

15. (a) The Secretary shall be the Principal Executive Officer of the Authority and shall exercise his powers and perform his duties under the control of the Chairperson.

    (b) The Authority, in the discharge of its functions under the Act, may take such assistance from the Secretary as it may deem fit.

    (c) In particular, and without prejudice to the generality of the provisions of sub-regulations (a) and (b) of this regulation, the Secretary shall have the following powers and perform the following duties, viz:-

    (i) He shall have custody of the records and the seal of the Authority.

    (ii) He shall receive or cause to receive all documents, including, inter alia, complaints, applications or reference pertaining to the Authority.

    (iii) He shall scrutinize documents, including, inter alia, complaints, applications or references and shall be entitled to seek clarifications or rectifications upon the same and issue appropriate directions pertaining to the acceptance or rejection of such documents.

(iv) He shall prepare or cause to be prepared briefs and summaries of pleadings presented by various parties in cases filed before the Authority.

(v) He shall carry out such functions under the Act and the Rules, as may be delegated to him by the Chairperson, by general or special order.

(vi) He shall assist the Authority in the proceedings relating to the powers exercisable by the Authority, as directed by the Chairperson.

(vii) He shall provide notice for meeting, prepare the agenda for meetings and minute the proceedings of the Authority's meetings.

(viii) He shall authenticate the orders passed by the Authority.

(ix) He shall, so far as it is possible, monitor compliance of the orders passed by the Authority and shall forthwith bring to the notice of the Authority any non-compliance thereof.

(x) He shall have the right to collect from the State Government or local authorities or other offices, companies and firms or any other party as may be directed by the Chairperson, such information and record, report, documents, etc. as may be considered necessary for the purpose of efficient discharge of the functions of the Authority under the Act and the Rules and place the same before the Authority.

16. In the absence of the Secretary, the Officer of the Authority designated by the Chairperson in this behalf shall exercise the powers and discharge the functions of the Secretary.

17. The Chairperson shall, at all times, have the power, either on an application made by any interested or affected party or suo motu, to review, revoke, revise, modify, amend, alter or otherwise change any order issued or action taken by the Secretary or any Officer of the Authority, if considered appropriate.

18. The Secretary may, with the written approval of the Chairperson, delegate to any Officer of the Authority any function required by these Regulations or otherwise to be exercised by the Secretary.

Meetings of the Authority:-

19. The provision contained in Regulations 20, 21, 22, 23 and 24 shall be applicable to the meetings of the Authority, other than the adjudicatory proceedings of the Authority.

20. The quorum for the meetings of the Authority shall be two.

21. If in any meeting of the Authority duly convened, the quorum is not present, the meeting shall stand adjourned for the next suitable date & time and place as decided by the Authority.

22. The Chairperson shall preside over the meetings and conduct the business. Members stationed at Benches, outside Ahmedabad/Gandhinagar, may participate in the meetings through video conferencing. If the Chairperson is unable to be present in the meetings for any reason, or where there is no Chairperson, the Members present shall decide on mutual consent the member to preside at the meeting.

23. (a) All questions which come up before any meetings of the Authority shall be decided by a majority of votes of the Members present and voting. In the event of an equality of votes, the Chairperson or in his absence, the Member presiding shall have a second or casting vote.

    (b) Save as otherwise provided in these Regulations, every Member shall have one vote.

24. (a) The Secretary or in his absence an Officer of the Authority designated by the Chairperson, shall record the minutes of the meetings and maintain a register which will, amongst other things, contain the names and designation of Members and invitees present in the meeting, a record of proceedings and notes of dissent, if any. In case of dissent the draft minutes shall, as soon as practicable, be sent to the Chairperson and the attending Members.

    (b) The decision taken in a meeting of the Authority shall be recorded in the minutes in a clear and concise manner, along with reasons. In case the minutes record any statement/submission made by an invitee, a copy of the minutes shall be sent to such invitee.

Adjudication Proceedings before the Authority: -

25. For adjudication proceedings with respect to complaints filed other than the matters fall under sections 12, 14, 18 and 29 of the Act with the Authority, the

Authority may, by general order or specific order, direct that specific matters or issues be heard and decided by a single bench of either the Chairperson or any Member of the Authority.

Vacancies, etc., not to invalidate proceedings:

26. No act or proceedings of the Authority shall be questioned or shall be invalidated merely on the ground of existence of any vacancy or defect in the construction of the Authority.

Authorized Representative:

27. A person who is a party to any proceedings before the Authority may either appear in person or authorise any other person to present his case before the Authority and to do all or any of the acts for the purpose.

    Provided that the person appearing on behalf of any person in any proceeding before the Authority shall file a Memorandum of Authorisation, in Form 6 herein.

    Provided further that for matters pertaining to Rule 6(1) of the Gujarat Real Estate (Regulation and Development) (General) Rules 2017, the Authority may, from time to time, determine the terms and conditions subject to which the allottees may authorise representative(s) to plead on their behalf. In such cases the Authority shall have the power to summon and enforce the attendance of all persons who are concerned with the Real Estate Project, including lenders, as well as the persons who have accorded permissions to the Real Estate Project, as Competent Authority.

Orders of the Authority:

28. The Authority, Chairperson or Members as the case may be hearing a proceeding shall pass orders in such proceedings, and such orders shall be signed by the Chairperson, Members or as the case may be the Authority hearing such proceeding. Every order shall be a in writing recording reasons for it.

29. All orders and decisions shall be certified by the signature of the Secretary or an Officer empowered in this behalf by the Chairperson and shall bear the official seal of the Authority and be communicated as expeditiously as possible from the date of passing thereof to all parties in the proceeding.

Records of the Authority:-

30. The Authority shall maintain an indexed database of its records including, inter alia, complaints filed, details of hearings conducted, orders/documents issued from time to time.

31. (a) Subject to sub-regulation (c) herein, records of the Authority shall be open to inspection by all, subject to the payment of the fee and complying with the terms as the Authority may direct.

    (b) The authority shall, on such terms and conditions as the Authority considers appropriate, provide for supply of certified copies of documents and papers available with the Authority to any person, applying in Form 7, subject to the payment of fee and complying with the terms as the Authority may direct. The Authority shall designate an Officer for ensuring timely response to requests received for supply of certified copies of documents who shall endeavour to dispatch the certified copies of documents requested for within a period of twenty one (21) working days from the date of receipt of request.

    (c) The Authority may, by order, direct that any information, documents and papers/materials maintained by the Authority, shall be confidential or privileged and shall not be available for inspection or supply of certified copies, and the Authority may also direct that such document, papers, or materials shall not be used in any manner except as specifically authorized by the Authority.

32. The Authority shall endeavour to make information involving public interest accessible and available to the public, including, inter alia, through its website.

Interim Orders, Investigation, Inquiry, collection of information, etc.:

33. The Authority may pass such ad-interim or interim orders, as the Authority may consider appropriate at any stage of any proceedings, having regard to the facts and circumstances of the case.

34. The Authority may make such direction or order as it thinks fit for collection of information, inquiry, investigation, entry, search, seizure and without prejudice to the generality of its powers, including, inter alia, the following:-

   (a) The Authority may, at any time, direct the Secretary or any one or more Officers or any other person as the Authority considers appropriate to study, investigate or furnish information with respect to any matter within the jurisdiction of the Authority under the Act and the Rules.
   (b) The Authority may, for the above purpose, give such other directions as it may deem fit and state the time within which the report is to be submitted or information furnished.
   (c) The Authority may issue or authorise the Secretary or an Officer to issue directions to any person to produce before it and allow to be examined and kept by an Officer of the Authority directed in this behalf the books, accounts, etc., or to furnish any information to the designated Officer.
   (d) The Authority may issue such directions, for the purpose of collection of any information, particulars or documents that the Authority considers necessary in connection with the discharge of its functions under the Act and the Rule.
   (e) If any such report or information obtained appears to the Authority to be insufficient or inadequate, the Authority or the Secretary or an Officer authorised for the purpose may give directions for further inquiry, report and furnishing of information.
   (f) The Authority may direct such incidental, consequential and supplemental matters to be attended to which may be considered relevant in connection with the above.

35. If the report or information obtained in accordance with Regulation 33 above or any part thereof is proposed to be relied upon by the Authority for forming its opinion or view in any proceedings, the parties to the proceedings shall be given a reasonable opportunity for filling objections and making submissions on such report or information.

Confidentiality:

36. (a) The Authority shall appraise and determine whether any documents or evidence provided to it by any party and claimed by that party to be of a confidential nature merits being withheld from disclosure to other parties as being confidential and shall provide brief reasons in writing for arriving at its conclusion.

(b) If the Authority is of the view that the claim for confidentiality is justified the Authority may direct that the same be not provided to such parties as the Authority may deem fit. However, the party claiming the confidentiality shall provide a brief non-confidential summary of the substance of the documents found to be confidential and the import of the same.

(c) Notwithstanding the above, it shall be open to the Authority to take into consideration the contents of the documents found to be confidential in arriving at its decision.

Review of decisions, directions, and orders:

37. (a) Any person aggrieved by a direction, decision or order of the Authority, from which (i) no appeal has been preferred or (ii) from which no appeal is allowed, may, upon the discovery of new and important matter or evidence which, after the exercise of due diligence, was not within his knowledge or could not be produced by him at the time when the direction, decision or order was passed or on account of some mistake or error apparent from the face of the record, or for any other sufficient reasons, may apply for a review of such order, within forty-five (45) days of the date of the direction, decision or order, as the case may be, to the Authority.

(b) An application for such review shall be filed in the same manner as a complaint under these Regulations.

(c) The Authority shall for the purposes of any proceedings for review of its decisions, directions and orders be vested with the same powers as are vested in a civil court under the Code of Civil Procedure, 1908.

(d) When it appears to the Authority that there is no sufficient ground for review, the Authority shall reject such review application.

(e) When the Authority is of the opinion that the review application should be granted, it shall grant the same provided that no such application will be granted without previous notice to the opposite side or party to enable him to appear and to be heard in support of the decision or order, the review of which is applied for.

Continuance of Proceedings after death, etc.

38. (a) Where in a proceeding, any of the parties to the proceeding dies or is adjudicated as an insolvent or in the case of a company under liquidation/winding up, the proceeding shall continue with the other partners, successors-in-interest, the executor, administrator, receiver, liquidator or other legal representative of the party concerned, as the case may be.

(b) The Authority may, for reasons to be recorded, treat the proceedings as abated in case the Authority so directs and dispense with the need to bring the successors-in-interest on the record of the case.

(c) In case any person wishes to bring on record the successors-in-interest, etc., the application for the purpose shall be filed within ninety (90) days from the event requiring the successors-in-interest to be brought on record. The Authority may condone the delay, if any, for sufficient reasons.

Issue of orders and directions:

39. Subject to the provisions of the Act, Rules and Regulations, the Authority may, from time to time issue orders and directions in regard to the implementation of the Regulations and procedure to be followed as it deems fit.

Saving of Inherent power of the Authority:

40. Nothing in the Regulations shall be deemed to limit or otherwise affect the inherent power of the Authority to make such orders as may be necessary for meeting the ends of justice or to prevent the abuse of the process of the Authority.

41   Nothing in these Regulations shall bar the Authority from adopting in conformity with the provisions of the Act or Rules, a procedure, which is at variance with any of the provisions of these Regulations including summary procedures, if the Authority, in view of the special circumstance of a matter or class of matters and for reasons to be recorded in writing, deems it necessary or expedient for so dealing with such a matter or class of matters.

42.   Nothing in the Regulations shall bar the Authority to deal with any matter or exercise any power under the Act or Rules for which no regulations have been framed, and the Authority may deal with such matters, powers and functions in a manner it thinks fit.

General power to amend/rectify:

43.   The Authority may, at any time and on such terms as to costs or otherwise, as it may think fit, amend any defect or error in any proceedings before it (including any clerical or arithmetical error in any order passed by the Authority), and all necessary amendments, rectifications shall be made for the purpose of determining the real question or issue arising in the proceedings.

Provided that if the Authority desires to make amendments or rectifications in order to determine the real question or issue arising the Authority shall provide an opportunity to the parties affected by such amendment or rectification touching the real question or issue to make representations and submissions with respect to the proposed amendment or rectification.

Power to remove difficulties:

44.   If any difficulty arises in giving effect to any of the provisions of the Regulations, the Authority may, by general or special order, do anything not being inconsistent with the provisions of the Act or Rules, which appears to be necessary or expedient for the purpose of removing the difficulties.

Extension or abridgement of time prescribed:

45. Subject to the provisions of the Act or the Rules, the time prescribed by the Regulations or by order of the Authority for doing any act may be extended (whether it has already expired or not) or abridged for sufficient reason by an order of the Authority.

Costs:

46. (a) Subject to such condition and limitation as may be directed by the Authority, the costs of and incidental to, all proceedings shall be awarded at the discretion of the Authority and the Authority shall have full power to determine by whom or out of what funds and to what extent such costs are to be paid and give all necessary directions for the aforesaid purposes.

(b) The costs shall be paid within thirty (30) days from the date of the order or within such time as the Authority may, by order, direct. If a party fails to comply with an order for costs within the permitted period, the order of the Authority awarding costs shall be executed forthwith in the same manner as a decree/order of a Civil Court.

Administrative Charges and Standard Fees:

47. The Authority may, by order, fix standard fees, to be levied on the promoters or real estate agents or allottees for inspection of documents, certified copies of documents, the updating of website, database management and maintenance of the Website.

FORM 1

ARCHITECT'S CERTIFICATE

(To be submitted at the time of Registration of Ongoing Project and for withdrawal of Money from Designated Account)

Date:

To

The_____ (Name & Address of Promoter).

Subject: Certificate of Percentage of Completion of Construction Work of _____No. of Building(s)_____Wing(s) of the _____Phase of the Project (Gujarat RERA Registration Number) situated on the Plot bearing C.N. No/CTS No./Survey no./Final Plot no_____ demarcated by its boundaries (latitude and longitude of the end points)_____to the North _____to the South _____ to the East _____to the West of Division _____village _____ taluka _____District _____ PIN _____ admeasuring _____ sq.mts. area being developed by (Promoter's Name)

Sir,

I/We _____ have undertaken assignment as Architect/Engineer of certifying Percentage of Completion of Construction Work of the _____Building(s)/_____Wing(s) of the _____Phase of the Project, situated on the plot bearing C.N. No./CTS No./Survey no./Final Plot no._____ of Division _____ village _____ taluka _____ District _____ PIN _____ admeasuring _____ sq.mts. area being developed by (Promoter's Name) as per the approved plan.

1. Following technical professionals are appointed by Owner/Promoter:- (as applicable)
    (i)   M/s./Shri/Smt._____ as Architect/Engineer
    (ii)   M/s./Shri/Smt._____ as Structural Consultant
    (iii) M/s./Shri/Smt._____ as MEP Consultant
    (iv) M/s./Shri/Smt._____ as Site Supervisor/Clerk of Works

Based on Site Inspection, with respect to each of the Building/Wing of the aforesaid Real Estate Project, I certify that as on the date of this certificate, the Percentage of Work done for each of the building/Wing of the Real Estate Project as registered vide number _____ under GujRERA is as per table A herein below. The percentage of the work executed with respect to each of the activity of the entire phase is detailed in Table A and B.

Table – A

Building/Wing Number _____ (to be prepared separately for each Building/Wing of the Project)

Sr. No.	Tasks/Activity	Percentage of work done
1	Excavation	
2	_____ number of Basement(s) and Plinth	
3	_____ number of Podiums	
4	Stilt Floor	
5	_____ number of Slabs of Super Structure	
6	Internal walls, Internal Plaster, Floorings within Flats/Premises, Doors and Windows to each of the Flat/Premises	
7	Sanitary Fittings within the Flat/Premises	
8	Staircases, Lifts Wells and Lobbies at each Floor level connecting Staircases and Lifts, Overhead and Underground Water Tanks	
9	The external plumbing and external plaster, elevation, completion of terraces with waterproofing of the Building/Wing.	
10	Installation of lifts, water pumps, Fire Fighting Fittings and Equipment as per CFO NOC, Electrical fittings to Common Areas, electro, mechanical equipment, compliance to conditions of environment/CRZ NOC, Finishing to entrance lobby/s, plinth protection, paving of areas appurtenant to Building/Wing, Compound Wall and all other requirements as may be required to Obtain Occupation/Completion Certificate	

TABLE-B

Internal & External Development Works in Respect of the entire Registered Phase

Sr. No.	Common areas and Facilities Amenities	Proposed (Yes/No)	Percentage of Work Done	Remarks
1	Internal Roads & Footpaths			
2	Water Supply			
3	Sewerage (chamber, lines, Septic Tank, STP)			
4	Storm Water Drains			
5	Landscaping & Tree Planting			
6	Street Lighting			
7	Community Buildings			
8	Treatment and disposal of sewage and sullage water /STP			
9	Solid Waste Management & Disposal			
10	Water Conservation, Rain Water Harvesting, Percolating Well/Pit			
11	Energy Management			
12	Fire Protection and Fire Safety Requirements			
13	Electrical Meter Room, Sub-station, Receiving Station			
14	Others (Option to Add more)			

Yours Faithfully,

Signature & Name (IN BLOCK LETTERS) OF Architect/Engineer
(License No............)

FORM – 2

ENGINEER'S CERTIFICATE

(To be submitted at the time of Registration of Ongoing Project and for withdrawal of Money from Designated Account – Project wise)

Date:

To

The _____ (Name & Address of Promoter),

Subject: Certificate of Cost Incurred for Development of (Project Name) for Construction of _____building(s)_____Wing(s) of the _____ phase (GujRERA Registration Number) situated on the Plot bearing C.N. No./CTS No./Survey no./Final Plot no. _____.

Demarcated by its boundaries (latitude and longitude of the end points)

_____to the North _____ to the South _____ to the East _____ to the West of Division _____ village _____ taluka _____ District _____ PIN _____ admeasuring _____ sq.mts. area being developed by (Promoter)

Ref: GujRERA Registration Number _____

Sir,

I/We_____ have undertaken assignment of certifying Estimated Cost for the Real Estate Project proposed to be registered under GujRERA, being _____Building(s)/_____ Wing(s) of the _____ Phase situated on the plot bearing C.N. No/CTS No./Survey no./Final Plot no._____ of Division _____ village _____ taluka _____ District _____ PIN _____ admeasuring _____ sq.mts. area being developed by (Owner/Promoter)

1. Following technical professionals are appointed by Owner/Promoter:- (as applicable)
    - (i) M/s/Shri/Smt_____ as Architect/Engineer
    - (ii) M/s/Shri/Smt_____ as Structural Consultant
    - (iii) M/s/Shri/Smt_____ as MEP Consultant
    - (iv) M/s/Shri/Smt_____ as Quantity Surveyor*

2. We have estimated the cost of the completion to obtain Occupation Certificate/Completion Certificate, of the Civil, MEP and Allied works, of the Building(s) of the project. Our estimated cost calculations are based on the Drawing/Plans made available to us for the project under reference by the Developer and Consultants and the Schedule of items and quantity for the entire work as calculated by _____ quantity Surveyor* appointed by Developer/Engineer and the site inspection carried out by us.

3. We estimate Total Estimated Cost of completion of the building(s) of the aforesaid project under reference as Rs._____ (Total of Table A and B). The estimated Total Cost of Project is with reference to the Civil, MEP and allied works required to be completed for the purpose of obtaining occupation certificate/completion certificate for the building(s) from the _____ being the Planning Authority under whose jurisdiction the aforesaid project is being implemented.

4. The Estimated Cost Incurred till date is calculated at Rs._____ (Total of Table A and B). The amount of Estimated Cost Incurred is calculated on the base of amount of Total Estimated Cost.

5. The Balance Cost of Completion of the Civil, MEP and Allied works of the Building(s) of the subject project to obtain Occupation Certificate/Completion Certificate from _____ (Planning Authority) is estimated at Rs._____ (Total of Table A and B).

6. I certify that the Cost of the Civil, MEP and allied work for the aforesaid Project as completed on the date of this certificate is as given in Table A and B below;

TABLE – A

Building/Wing bearing Number _____ or called _____

(to be prepared separately for each Building/Wing of the Real Estate Project)

Sr. No.	Particulars	Amounts (in Rs.)
1	Total Estimated Cost of the building/wing as on _____ date of Registration is	
2	Cost incurred as on _____	
3	Work done in Percentage (as Percentage of the estimated cost)	
4	Balance Cost to be Incurred (Based on Estimated Cost)	
5	Cost Incurred on Additional/Extra Items as on _____ not included in the Estimated Cost (Table –C)	

TABLE – B

(to be prepared for the entire registered phase of the Real Estate Project)

Sr. No.	Particulars	Amounts (in Rs.)
1	Total Estimated Cost of the Internal and External Development Works including amenities and Facilities in the layout as on _____ date of Registration is	
2	Cost incurred as on _____	
3	Work done in Percentage (as Percentage of the estimated cost)	
4	Balance Cost to be Incurred (Based on Estimated Cost)	
5	Cost Incurred on Additional/Extra Items as on _____ not included in the Estimated Cost (Table –C)	

Yours Faithfully,

Signature of Engineer

(Licence No...................)

*Note

1. The scope of work is to complete entire Real Estate Project as per drawings approved from time to time so as to obtain Occupation Certificate/Completion Certificate.
2. (*) Quantity Survey can be done by office of Engineer or can be done by an independent Quantity Surveyor, whose certificate of quantity calculated can be relied upon by the Engineer. In case of independent quantity surveyor being appointed by Promoter, the name has to be mentioned at the place marked (*) and in case quantity are being calculated by office of Engineer, the name of the person in the office of Engineer, who is responsible for the quantity calculated should be mentioned at the place marked (*).
3. The estimated cost includes all labour, material, equipment and machinery required to carry out entire work.
4. As this is an estimated cost, any deviation in quantity required for development of the Real Estate Project will result in amendment of the cost incurred/to be incurred.
5. All components of work with specifications are indicative and not exhaustive.

Table –C
List of Extra/Additional Items executed with Cost
(Which were not part of the original Estimate of Total Cost)

FORM-3

CHARTERED ACCOUNTS CERTIFICATE (On Letter Head)

(FOR REGISTRATION OF A PROJECT AND SUBSEQUENT WITHDRAWL OF MONEY)

Cost of Real Estate Project GujRERA Registration Number _____

Sr. No.	Particulars	Amount (in Rs.)	
		Estimated (Colum -A)	**Incurred & Paid** (Colum -B)
1	**i. Land Cost:** a. Acquisition Cost of Land or Development Rights, lease Premium, lease rent, interest cost incurred or payable on Land Cost and legal cost b. Amount of Premium payable to obtain development rights, FSI, additional FSI, fungible area and any other incentive under DCR from Local Authority or State Government or any Statutory Authority c. Acquisition cost of TDR (if any) d. Amounts payable to State Government or competent authority or any other statutory authority of the State or Central Government towards stamp duty, transfer charges, registration fees etc. and e. Land Premium payable as per annual statement of rates (ASR) for redevelopment of land owned by Public Authorities. f. Under Rehabilitation Scheme: (i) Estimated construction cost of rehab building including site development and infrastructure for the same as certified by Engineer (Column-A) (ii) Actual Cost of construction of rehab building incurred as per the books of accounts as verified by the CA (Column-B) **Note: (for total cost of construction incurred, Minimum of (i) or (ii) is to be considered)**		

	(iii) Cost towards clearance of land of all or any encumbrances including cost of removal of legal/illegal occupants, cost for providing temporary transit accommodation or rent in lieu of Transit Accommodation, overhead cost. (iv) Cost of ASR linked premium, fees, charges and security deposits or maintenance deposit, or any amount whatsoever payable to any authorities towards and in project of rehabilitation.		
	Sub-Total of LAND COST		

		Amount (in Rs.)	
		Estimated **(Colum -A)**	**Incurred & Paid** **(Colum -B)**
ii.	**Development Cost/Cost of Construction:** a. (i) Estimated Cost of Construction as certified by Engineer (Column - A) (ii) Actual Cost of Construction incurred as per the books of accounts as verified by the CA (Column - B) **Note: (for adding to total cost of construction incurred, Minimum of (i) or (ii) is to be considered)** (iii) On-site expenditure for development of entire project excluding cost of construction as per (i) or (ii) above, i.e. salaries, consultants fees, site overheads, development works, cost of services (including water, electricity, sewerage, drainage, layout roads etc.), cost of machineries and equipment including its hire and maintenance costs, consumables etc. All costs directly incurred to complete		

		the construction of the entire phase of the project registered. b. Payment of Taxes, cess, fees, charges, premiums, interest etc. to any Statutory Authority. c. Interest payable to financial institutions, scheduled banks, non-banking financial institution (NBFC) or money lenders on construction funding or money borrowed for construction:		
		Sub-Total of Development Cost		

2. **Total Estimated Cost of the Real Estate Project**
   (1 (i) + 1 (ii) of Estimated Column -A

3. **Total Cost Incurred and Paid of the Real Estate Project**
   (1 (i) + 1 (ii) of Incurred Column - B

4. Percentage of completion of Construction Work
   (as per Project Architect's Certificate on completion of project) _____ %

5. Proportion of the Cost incurred on Land Cost and Construction Cost to the Total Estimated Cost.(3/2) _____%

6. Amount which can be withdrawn from the Designated Account
   Total Estimated Cost *Proportion of cost incurred and paid
   (Sr. number 2 *Sr. number 5)

7. Less: Amount withdrawn till date of this certificate as per the Books of Accounts and Bank Statement

8. Net Amount which can be withdrawn from the Designated Bank Account under this certificate

   This certificate is being issued for RERA compliance for the Company (Promoter's Name) and is based on the records and documents produced before me and explanations provided to me by the management of the Company.

   Yours Faithfully,

   Signature of Chartered Accountant
   (Membership Number......................)
    _____
   Name

(ADDITIONAL INFORMATION FOR ONGOING PROJECTS)

1. Estimated Balance Cost to Complete the Real Estate Project   _____
   (Difference of Total Estimated Project cost less Cost incurred)

2. Balance amount of receivables from sold apartments
   as per Annexure-A to this certificate
   (as certified by Chartered Accountant as verified from the records
   And books of Accounts)

3. (i) Balance Unsold area
       to be certified by Management and to be verified by CA from the
       records and books of accounts)

   (ii) Estimated amount of sales proceeds in respect of unsold apartments
        as per Annexure-A to this certificate.

4. Estimated receivables of ongoing project. Sum of 2 + 3 (ii)

5. Amount to be deposited in Designated Account – 70% or 100%
   If 4 is greater than 1, then 70% of the balance receivables of
   Ongoing project will be deposited in designated Account.
   If 4 is lesser than 1, then 100% of the balance receivables of
   Ongoing project will be deposited in designated Account.   %
                                                                        _____

This certificate is being issued for RERA compliance for the Company (Promoter's Name) and is based on the records and documents produced before me and explanations provided to me by the management of the Company.

Yours Faithfully,

Signature of Chartered Accountant
(Membership Number......................)

_____
Name

Annexure-A

Statement for calculation of Receivables from the Sales of the Ongoing Real Estate Project:

Sold Inventory

Sr.No.	Flat No.	Carpet Area (in sq.mts.)	Unit Consideration as per Agreement/Letter of Allotment	Received Amount	Balance Amount

(Unsold Inventory Valuation)

Of the Residential/commercial premises Rs. _____ per sm.

Sr. No.	Flat No.	Carpet Area (in sq. mts.)	Unit Consideration

FORM-4

ARCHITECT'S CERTIFICATE

(To be issued on completion of each of the Building/Wing)

Date:

To

The _____ (Name & Address of Promoter),

Subject: Certificate of Completion of Construction Work of _____Building/_____Wing of the Building of the Project (GujRERA Registration Number) situated on the Plot bearing C.N. No/CTS No./Survey no./Final Plot no_____ demarcated by its boundaries (latitude and longitude of the end points)_____to the North_____ to the South _____ to the East _____ to the West of Division _____ village _____ taluka _____ District _____PIN_____ admeasuring _____ sq.mts. area being developed by Promoter's Name) _____.

Sir,

I/We _____ have undertaken assignment as Architect/Engineer of certifying completion of Construction Work of _____Building/_____ Wing of the Building situated on the plot bearing C.N. No.CTS No./Survey no./Final Plot no _____ of Division _____ village _____ taluka _____ District _____ PIN _____ admeasuring _____ sq.mts. area being developed by (Promoter's Name)

2. Following technical professionals are appointed by Owner/Promoter:- (as applicable)

    (i)   M/s/Shri/Smt. _____ as Architect/Engineer
    (ii)   M/s/Shri/Smt. _____ as Structural Consultant
    (iii)   M/s/Shri/Smt. _____ as MEP Consultant
    (iv)   M/s/Shri/Smt._____ as Site Supervisor/Clerk of Works

3.	Based on Completion Certificate received from Structural Engineer and Site Supervisor/Clerks of Works and to the best of my/our knowledge I/We hereby certify that _____ Building/_____wing of the Building has been completed in all aspects and is fit for occupancy for which it has been erected/re-erected/constructed and enlarged. The _____Building/_____wing of the Building is granted Occupancy Certificate/Completion Certificate bearing number_____ dated _____ by _____ (Local Planning Authority) .

Yours Faithfully,

Signature & Name (IN BLOCK LETTERS) of L.S/Architect with (License No......................)

FORM 5

ON THE LETTER HEAD OF CHARTERED ACCOUNTANT (WHO IS STATUTORY AUDITOR OF THE PROMOTER'S COMPANY/FIRM)

ANNUAL REFPORT ON STATEMENT OF ACCOUNTS

To (NAME & ADDRESS OF PROMOTER)

SUBJECT: Report on Statement of Accounts on project fund utilization and withdrawal by (Promoter) for the period from _____ to _____ with respect to GujRERA Regn. Number_____

1. This certificate is issued in accordance with the provisions of the Real Estate (Regulation and Development) Act, 2016 read along with the Gujarat Real Estate (Regulation and Development) Rules, 2017.

2. I/We have obtained all necessary information and explanation from the Company, during the course of our audit, which in my/our opinion are necessary for the purpose of this certificate.

3. I/We hereby confirm that I/We have examined the prescribed registers, books and documents and the relevant records of (Promoter) for the period ended _____ and hereby certify that:

    i. M/s. _____ (Promoter) have completed % of the project titled _____(Name) GujRERA Regn. No_____ located at _____

    ii. Amount collected during the year for this project is Rs._____ and amounts collected till date is Rs._____

    iii. Amount withdrawn during the year for this project is Rs._____ and amount withdrawn till date is Rs._____

4. I/We certify that the (Name of Promoter) has utilized the amounts collected for _____ project has been in accordance with the proportion to the percentage of completion of the project. (If not, please specify the amount withdrawn in excess of eligible amount or any other exceptions)

(Signature and Stamps/Seal of the Signatory CA)

Name of the Signatory:

Place:
Date:

Full Address

Membership No.:

Contact No.:   E mail

Form 6

(See Regulation 27)

BEFORE THE GUJARAT REAL ESTATE REGULATORY AUTHORITY

Authorisation Form

Complaint No./ _____ .

In the matter of

……………………………………………….. Petitioner

V/s …………………………………………. Respondent(s)

Memo of Authorisation

I/We, …………………. the petitioner/respondent abovenamed do hereby nominate, appoint and constitute……………………………………. to act, plead and appear on my/our behalf in the aforesaid matter.

IN WITNESS WHREOF I/We have set and subscribed my/our hands to this writing on this………….day of…………….

Place:_____   Signature

(Petitioner/Respondent)

Date:_____

Address for Correspondence

I/We accept ……………………………….

Form 7

(See Regulation 31)

BEFORE THE GUJARAT REAL ESTATE REGULATORY AUTHORITY

Application for inspection/obtaining copies of documents/records

I hereby apply for grant of permission to inspect/obtain copies of the following documents/records in the above case. The details are as follows:

1. Name & Address of the person seeking permission to inspect/obtain copies of the documents/records.
2. Whether he is party to the case or he is the authorised representative of any party. (Furnish necessary particulars).
3. Details of papers/documents sought to be inspected/copies required.
4. Date and duration of the inspection sought.
5. The amount of fee payable (as per relevant Regulations) and the mode of payment.

Place:

Date: Signature

Office Use

Granted inspection on_____/Rejected

Granted copies of documents on _____/ Rejected

Secretary/Officer/Nominee of the Authority
....

Secretary, GujRERA.

Dr. Manjula Subramaniam
Gujarat Real Estate Regulatory Authority

Annexure 'A'
Model Form of Agreement to be entered into between Promoter and Allottee(s) (See rule 9)

EXPLANATORY NOTE

This is a model form of Agreement, which may be modified and adapted in each case having regard to the facts and circumstances of respective case but in any event, matter and substance mentioned in those clauses, which are in accordance with the statute and mandatory according to the provisions of the Act shall be retained in each and every Agreement executed between the Promoter and Allottee. Any clause in this agreement found contrary to or inconsistent with any provisions of the Act, Rules and Regulations would be void *ab-initio*.

Model Form of Agreement

This Agreement made at............this.........day of.......... in the year Two Thousand and..................... between ....having address at ....hereinafter referred to as "the Promoter of the One Part and (.........................) having address at ....hereinafter referred to as " the Allottee" (...........................) of the Other Part.

WHEREAS by an Agreement/Conveyance dated ....day of.............20....... and executed between .... of the One Part (hereinafter referred to as " the Vendor") and the Promoter of the Other Part, the Vendor agreed with the Promoter for the absolute sale to the Promoter/sold absolutely to the Promoter an immovable property being piece or parcel of freehold land bearing Survey No. .... lying and being survey no. at .... in the Registration sub-District of .... admeasuring .... sq. mts. or thereabouts more particularly described in the First Schedule hereunder written (hereinafter referred to as "the project land").

OR

WHEREAS by and under a Lease / an Agreement for Lease dated the .... day of.................20....... made between .... of the One Part (hereinafter referred to as " the Lessor") and the Promoter of the Other Part, the Lessor agreed to grant unto the Promoter a lease in perpetuity/for a term of .... years in respect of a piece or parcel of leasehold land bearing situate at ...., admeasuring........sq.m. or thereabouts more particularly described in the First Schedule hereunder written (hereinafter referred to as " the project land") at a rent of Rs........... per annum/month and on the terms and conditions contained in the said Lease Deed/Agreement for Lease.

AND WHEREAS the lease Deed/Agreement for Lease, is with the benefit and right to construct any new building/s if so permitted by the concerned local authority.

OR

WHEREAS by an Agreement dated ....day of 20......./Power of Attorney dated............. executed between Shri............... (hereinafter referred to as "the Original Owner") of the One Part and the Promoter of the Other Part (hereinafter referred to as "the Development Agreement"), the Original Owner granted to the Promoter development rights to the piece or parcel of freehold land lying and being at .... in the Registration Sub-District of.................. admeasuring .... sq. mts., or thereabouts more particularly described in the First Schedule therein as well as in the First Schedule hereunder written (hereinafter referred to as "the project land') and to construct thereon building/s in accordance with the terms and conditions contained in the Development Agreement/Power of Attorney;

OR

(Give Complete Recital of the Title of the Promoter to the plot on which promoter proposes to construct and sale the Apartment)

AND WHEREAS the Promoters are entitled and enjoined upon to construct buildings on the project land;

AND WHEREAS the Vendor/Lessor/Original Owner/Promoter is in possession of the project land

AND WHEREAS the Promoter has proposed to construct on the project land (here specify number of buildings and wings thereof) .... having _____(here specify number of Basements/podiums/stilt and upper floors)

AND WHEREAS the Allottee is offered an Apartment bearing number _____ on the_____ floor, (herein after referred to as the said "Apartment") in the _____ wing of the Building called _____ (herein after referred to as the said "Building") being constructed in the_____phase of the said project, by the Promoter

AND WHEREAS the Promoter has registered the Project under the provisions of the Act with the Real Estate Regulatory Authority at _____ no_____; authenticated copy is attached in Annexure 'B';

AND WHEREAS by virtue of the Development Agreement/Power of Attorney the Promoter has sole and exclusive right to sell the Apartments in the said building/s to be constructed by the Promoter on the project land and to enter into Agreement/s with the allottee(s)/s of the Apartments to receive the sale consideration in respect thereof;

AND WHEREAS on demand from the allottee, the Promoter has given inspection to the Allottee of all the documents of title relating to the project land and the plans, designs and specifications prepared by the Promoter's Architects Messrs................................... and of such other documents as are specified under the Real Estate (Regulation and Development) Act, 2016 (hereinafter referred to as "the said Act") and the Rules and Regulations made thereunder and the Allottee if satisfied in respect of the same;

AND WHEREAS the authenticated copies of Certificate of Title issued by the attorney at law or advocate of the Promoter, authenticated copies of Property card or extract of Village Forms VI and VII and XII or any other relevant revenue record showing the nature of the title of the Promoter to the project land on which the Apartments are constructed or are to be constructed have also been inspected by the Allottee and is satisfied in respect of the same.

AND WHEREAS the authenticated copies of the plans of the Layout as approved by the concerned Local Authority has been inspected by the Allottee.

AND WHEREAS the authenticated copies of the plans of the Layout as proposed by the Promoter and according to which the construction of the buildings and open spaces are proposed to be provided for on the said project has also been inspected by the Allottee,

AND WHEREAS the authenticated copies of the plans and specifications of the Apartment agreed to be purchased by the Allottee has been annexed and marked as Annexure A

AND WHEREAS the Promoter has got some of the approvals from the concerned local authority(s) to the plans, the specifications, elevations, sections and of the said building/s and shall obtain the balance approvals from various authorities from time to time, so as to obtain Building Completion Certificate or Occupancy Certificate of the said Building.

AND WHEREAS while sanctioning the said plans concerned local authority and/or Government has laid down certain terms, conditions, stipulations and restrictions which are to be observed and performed by the Promoter while developing the project land and the said building and upon due observance and performance of which only the completion or occupancy certificate in respect of the said building/s shall be granted by the concerned local authority.

AND WHEREAS the Promoter has accordingly commenced construction of the said building/s in accordance with the said proposed plans.

AND WHEREAS the Allottee has applied to the Promoter for allotment of an Apartment No. .... on .... floor in wing _____ situated in the building No. _____ being constructed in the _____ phase of the said Project,

AND WHEREAS the carpet area of the said Apartment is _____ square meters/square feet and "carpet area" means the net usable floor area of an apartment, excluding the area covered by the external walls, areas under services shafts, exclusive balcony or verandah area and exclusive open terrace area but includes the area covered by the internal partition walls of the apartment.

AND WHEREAS, the Parties relying on the confirmations, representations and assurances of each other to faithfully abide by all the terms, conditions and stipulations contained in this Agreement and all applicable laws, are now willing to enter into this Agreement on the terms and conditions appearing hereinafter;

AND WHEREAS, prior to the execution of these presents the Allottee has paid to the Promoter a sum of Rs..................... (Rupees ....) only, being part payment of the sale consideration of the Apartment agreed to be sold by the Promoter to the Allottee as advance payment or Application Fee (the payment and receipt whereof the Promoter both hereby admit and acknowledge) and the Allottee has agreed to pay to the Promoter the balance of the sale consideration in the manner hereinafter appearing.

AND WHEREAS, under section 13 of the said Act the Promoter is required to execute a written Agreement for sale of said Apartment with the Allottee, being in fact these presents and also to register said Agreement under the Registration Act, 1908.

In accordance with the terms and conditions set out in this Agreement and as mutually agreed upon by and between the Parties, the Promoter hereby agrees to sell and the Allottee hereby agrees to purchase the (Apartment/Plot) and the garage/covered parking(if applicable)

NOW THEREFOR, THIS AGREEMENT WITNESSETH AND IT IS HEREBY AGREED BY AND BETWEEN THE PARTIES HERETO AS FOLLOWS:-

1. The Promoter shall construct the said building/s consisting of .... basement and ground/ stilt, /................. podiums, and .... upper floors on the project land in accordance with the plans, designs and specifications as approved by the concerned local authority from time to time.

    Provided that the Promoter shall have to obtain prior consent in writing of the Allottee in respect of variations or modifications which may adversely affect the Apartment of the Allottee except any alteration or addition required by any Government authorities or due to change in law.

1(a) (i) The Allottee hereby agrees to purchase from the Promoter and the Promoter hereby agrees to sell to the Allottee Apartment No. .... of the type .... of carpet area admeasuring .... sq. metres/ sq. feet on .... floor in the building_____/wing (hereinafter referred to as "the Apartment") for the consideration of Rs. .... including Rs. .... being the proportionate price of the common areas and facilities appurtenant to the premises, the nature, extent and description of the common areas and facilities which are more particularly described in the Second Schedule annexed herewith. (the price of the Apartment including the proportionate price of the common areas and facilities and parking spaces should be shown separately).

(ii) The Allottee hereby agrees to purchase from the Promoter and the Promoter hereby agrees to sell to the Allottee balcony/verandha 1 having area admeasuring ……………..sq.metres/sq.feet forming part of the apartment for the consideration of Rs. _____/-

(iii) The Allottee hereby agrees to purchase from the Promoter and the Promoter hereby agrees to sell to the Allottee balcony/verandha 2 having area admeasuring ………………..sq.metres/sq.feet forming part of the apartment for the consideration Rs. _____/-

(iv) The Allottee hereby agrees to purchase from the Promoter and the Promoter hereby agrees to sell to the Allottee wash area balcony having area admeasuring ……….............sq.meters/sq. Feet forming part of the apartment for the consideration of of Rs. _____/-

(v) The Allottee hereby agrees to purchase from the Promoter and the Promoter hereby agrees to sell to the Allottee open terrace having area admeasuring .... sq.meters/sq. Feet forming part of the apartment for the consideration of of Rs. _____/-

(vi) The Allottee hereby agrees to purchase from the Promoter and the Promoter hereby agrees to sell to the Allottee open parking spaces bearing Nos _____ situated at _____ Basement and/or stilt and /or _____ podium being constructed in the layout for the consideration of Rs_____/-

(vii) The Allottee hereby agrees to purchase from the Promoter and the Promoter hereby agrees to sell to the Allottee covered parking spaces bearing Nos _____ situated at Basement and/or stilt and /or _____ podium being constructed in the layout for the consideration of Rs. _____/-.

1(b) The total aggregate consideration amount for the apartment mentioned herein above from clause 1 a (i) to (vii) is thus Rs._____/-

1(c) The Allottee has paid on or before execution of this agreement a sum of Rs _____ (Rupees _____ only) (not exceeding 10% of the total consideration) as advance payment or application fee and hereby agrees to pay to that Promoter the balance amount of Rs ....(Rupees ....) in the following manner :-

  i. Amount of Rs......../-(........) (not exceeding 30% of the total consideration) to be paid to the Promoter after the execution of Agreement

  ii. Amount of Rs......./-(..........) (not exceeding 45% of the total consideration) to be paid to the Promoter on completion of the Plinth of the building or wing in which the said Apartment is located.

  iii. Amount of Rs......./-(...........) (not exceeding 70% of the total consideration) to be paid to the Promoter on completion of the slabs including podiums and stilts of the building or wing in which the said Apartment is located.

  iv. Amount of Rs......./-(.............) (not exceeding 75% of the total consideration) to be paid to the Promoter on completion of the walls, internal plaster, floorings doors and windows of the said Apartment.

  v. Amount of Rs........./- (...........) (not exceeding 80% of the total consideration) to be paid to the Promoter on completion of the Sanitary fittings, staircases, lift wells, lobbies upto the floor level of the said Apartment.

  vi. Amount of Rs....../-(.....) (not exceeding 85% of the total consideration) to be paid to the Promoter on completion of the external plumbing and external plaster, elevation, terraces with waterproofing, of the building or wing in which the said Apartment is located.

  vii. Amount of Rs......./-(...........) (not exceeding 95% of the total consideration) to be paid to the Promoter on completion of the lifts, water pumps, electrical fittings, electro, mechanical and environment requirements, entrance lobby/s, plinth protection, paving of areas appertain and all other requirements as may be prescribed in the Agreement of sale of the building or wing in which the said Apartment is located.

  viii. Balance Amount of Rs...../-(............) against and at the time of handing over of the possession of the Apartment to the Allottee on or after receipt of occupancy certificate or completion certificate.

1(d) The total price as stated above excludes Taxes (consisting of tax paid or payable by the Promoter by way of Value Added Tax, Service Tax, and Cess or any other similar taxes which may be levied, in connection with the construction of and carrying out the Project payable by the Promoter) up to the date of handing over the possession of the [Apartment/Plot], which shall be separatelytpayable by the Allottee in the manner as may be decided by the Promoter.

1(e) The total price is escalation-free, save and except escalations/increases, due to increase on account of development charges payable to the competent authority and/or any other increase in charges which may be levied or imposed by the competent authority Local Bodies/Government from time to time. The Promoter undertakes and agrees that while raising a demand on the Allottee for increase in development charges, cost, or levies imposed by the competent authorities etc., the Promoter shall enclose the said notification/order/rule/regulation published/issued in that behalf to that effect along with the demand letter being issued to the Allottee, which shall only be applicable on subsequent payments.

1(f) The Promoter may allow, in its sole discretion, a rebate for early payments of equal instalments payable by the Allottee by discounting such early payments @ _____ % per annum for the period by which the respective instalment has been preponed. The provision for allowing rebate and such rate of rebate shall not be subject to any revision/withdrawal, once granted to an Allottee by the Promoter.

1(g) The Promoter shall confirm the final carpet area that has been allotted to the Allottee after the construction of the Building is complete and the occupancy certificate is granted by the competent authority, by furnishing details of the changes, if any, in the carpet area, subject to a variation cap of three percent. The total price payable for the carpet area shall be recalculated upon confirmation by the Promoter. If there is any reduction in the carpet area within the defined limit then Promoter shall refund the excess money paid by Allottee within forty-five days with annual interest at the rate of __%, from the date when such an excess amount was paid by the Allottee. If there is any increase in the carpet area allotted to Allottee, the Promoter shall demand additional amount from the Allottee as per the next milestone of the Payment Plan. All these monetary adjustments shall be made at the same rate per square meter as agreed in Clause 1(a) of this Agreement.

1(h) The Allottee authorizes the Promoter to adjust/appropriate all payments made by him/her under any head(s) of dues against lawful outstanding, if any, in his/her name as the Promoter may in its sole discretion deem fit and the Allottee undertakes not to object/demand/direct the Promoter to adjust his payments in any manner.

Note: Each of the instalments mentioned in the sub clause (ii) and (iii) shall be further subdivided into multiple instalments linked to number of basements/podiums/floors in case of multi-storied building /wing.

2.1 The Promoter hereby agrees to observe, perform and comply with all the terms, conditions, stipulations and restrictions if any, which may have been imposed by the concerned local authority at the time of sanctioning the said plans or thereafter and shall, before handing over possession of the Apartment to the Allottee, obtain from the concerned local authority occupancy and/or completion certificates in respect of the Apartment.

2.2 Time is essence for the Promoter as well as the Allottee. The Promoter shall abide by the time schedule for completing the project and handing over the [Apartment/Plot] to the Allottee and the common areas to the association of the allottees after receiving the occupancy certificate or the completion certificate or both, as the case may be.

Similarly, the Allottee shall make timely payments of the instalment and other dues payable by him/her and meeting the other obligations under the Agreement subject to the simultaneous completion of construction by the Promoter as provided in clause 1 (c) herein above. ("Payment Plan").

3. The Promoter hereby declares that the Floor Space Index available as on date in respect of the project land is .... square meters only and Promoter has planned to utilize Floor Space Index of _____ by availing of TDR or FSI available on payment of premiums or FSI available as incentive FSI by implementing various scheme as mentioned in the Development Control Regulation or based on expectation of increased FSI which may be available in future on modification to Development Control Regulations, which are applicable to the said Project. The Promoter has disclosed the Floor Space Index of _____ as proposed to be utilized by him on the project land in the said Project and Allottee has agreed to purchase the said Apartment based on the proposed construction and sale of apartments to be carried out by the Promoter by utilizing the proposed FSI and on the understanding that the declared proposed FSI shall belong to Promoter only.

4.1 If the Promoter fails to abide by the time schedule for completing the project and handing over the [Apartment/Plot] to the Allottee, the Promoter agrees to pay to the Allottee, who does not intend to withdraw from the project, interest at the rate of __% per annum, on all the amounts paid by the Allottee, for every month of delay, till the handing over of the possession. The Allottee agrees to pay to the Promoter, interest at the rate of __% per annum, on all the delayed payment which become due and payable by the Allottee to the Promoter under the terms of this Agreement from the date the said amount is payable by the allottee(s) to the Promoter.

4.2 Without prejudice to the right of promoter to charge interest in terms of sub clause 4.1 above, on the Allottee committing default in payment on due date of any amount due and payable by the Allottee to the Promoter under this Agreement (including his/her proportionate share of taxes levied by concerned local authority and other outgoings) and on the allottee committing three defaults of payment of instalments, the Promoter shall at his own option, may terminate this Agreement:

Provided that, Promoter shall give notice of fifteen days in writing to the Allottee, by Registered Post AD at the address provided by the allottee and mail at the e-mail address provided by the Allottee, of his intention to terminate this Agreement and of the specific breach or breaches of terms and conditions in respect of which it is intended to terminate the Agreement. If the Allottee fails to rectify the breach or breaches mentioned by the Promoter within the period of notice then at the end of such notice period, promoter shall be entitled to terminate this Agreement.

Provided further that upon termination of this Agreement as aforesaid, the Promoter shall refund to the Allottee (subject to adjustment and recovery of any agreed liquidated damages or any other amount which may be payable to Promoter) within a period of thirty days of the termination, the instalments of sale consideration of the Apartment which may till then have been paid by the Allottee to the Promoter.

5. The fixtures and fittings with regard to the flooring and sanitary fittings and amenities like one or more lifts with brand, or price range to be provided by the Promoter at his/her/its option in the said building and the Apartment as are set out in Annexure 'C', annexed hereto.

6. The Promoter shall give possession of the Apartment to the Allottee on or before................ day of ....20___. If the Promoter fails or neglects to give possession of the Apartment to the Allottee on account of reasons beyond his control and of his agents by the aforesaid date then the Promoter shall be liable on demand to refund to the Allottee the amounts already received by him in respect of the Apartment with interest at the same rate as may mentioned in the clause 4.1 herein above from the date the Promoter received the sum till the date the amounts and interest thereon is repaid.

Provided that the Promoter shall be entitled to reasonable extension of time for giving delivery of Apartment on the aforesaid date, if the completion of building in which the Apartment is to be situated is delayed on account of -
(i) war, civil commotion or act of God ;
(ii) any notice, order, rule, notification of the Government and/or other public or competent authority/court.

7.1 **Procedure for taking possession** - The Promoter, upon obtaining the occupancy certificate from the competent authority and the payment made by the Allottee as per the agreement shall offer in writing the possession of the [Apartment/Plot], to the Allottee in terms of this Agreement to be taken within 3 (three months from the date of issue of such notice and the Promoter shall give possession of the [Apartment/Plot] to the Allottee. The Promoter agrees and undertakes to indemnify the Allottee in case of failure of fulfilment of any of the provisions, formalities, documentation on part of the Promoter. The Allottee agree(s) to pay the maintenance charges as determined by the Promoter or association of allottees, as the case may be. The Promoter on its behalf shall offer the possession to the Allottee in writing within 7 days of receiving the occupancy certificate of the Project.

7.2 The Allottee shall take possession of the Apartment within 15 days of the written notice from the promotor to the Allottee intimating that the said Apartments are ready for use and occupancy:

7.3 **Failure of Allottee to take Possession of [Apartment/Plot]:** Upon receiving a written intimation from the Promoter as per clause 7.1, the Allottee shall take possession of the [Apartment/Plot] from the Promoter by executing necessary indemnities, undertakings and such other documentation as prescribed in this Agreement, and the Promoter shall give possession of the [Apartment/Plot] to the allottee. In case the Allottee fails to take possession within the time provided in clause 7.1 such Allottee shall continue to be liable to pay maintenance charges as applicable.

7.4 If within a period of five years from the date of handing over the Apartment to the Allottee, the Allottee brings to the notice of the Promoter any structural defect in the Apartment or the building in which the Apartment are situated or any defects on account of workmanship, quality or provision of service, then, wherever possible such defects shall be rectified by the Promoter at his own cost and in case it is not possible to rectify such defects, then the Allottee shall be entitled to receive from the Promoter, compensation for such defect in the manner as provided under the Act. Provided that the Promoter shall not be liable in respect of any structural defect or defects on account of workmanship, quality or provision of service which cannot be attributable to the Promoter or beyond the control of the Promoter.

8. The Allottee shall use the Apartment or any part thereof or permit the same to be used only for purpose of *residence/office/show-room/shop/godown for carrying on any industry or business.(*strike of which is not applicable) He shall use the garage or parking space only for purpose of keeping or parking vehicle.

9. The Allottee along with other allottee(s)s of Apartments in the building shall join in forming and registering the Society or Association or a Limited Company to be known by such name as the Promoter may decide and for this purpose also from time to time sign and execute the application for registration and/or membership and the other papers and documents necessary for the formation and registration of the Society or Association or Limited Company and for becoming a member, including the bye-laws of the proposed Society and duly fill in, sign and return to the Promoter within seven days of the same being forwarded by the Promoter to the Allottee, so as to enable the Promoter to register the common organisation of Allottee. No objection shall be taken by the Allottee if any, changes or modifications are made in the draft bye-laws, or the Memorandum and/or Articles of Association, as may be required by the Registrar of Co-operative Societies or the Registrar of Companies, as the case may be, or any other Competent Authority.

9.1 Within 15 days after notice in writing is given by the Promoter to the Allottee that the Apartment is ready for use and occupancy, the Allottee shall be liable to bear and pay the proportionate share (i.e. in proportion to the carpet area of the Apartment) of outgoings in respect of the project land and Building/s namely local taxes, betterment charges or such other levies by the concerned local authority and/or Government, water charges, insurance, common lights, repairs and salaries of clerks bill collectors, chowkidars, sweepers and all other expenses necessary and incidental to the management and maintenance of the project land and building/s. Until the Society or Limited Company is formed, the Allottee shall pay to the Promoter such proportionate share of outgoings as may be determined. The Allottee further agrees that till the Allottee's share is so determined the Allottee shall pay to the Promoter provisional monthly contribution of Rs. .... per month towards the outgoings. The amounts so paid by the Allottee to the Promoter shall not carry any interest and remain with the Promoter until the same is transferred to the society or the association or the limited company as aforesaid.

10. Over and above the amounts mentioned in the agreement to be paid by the Allottee, the Allottee shall on or before delivery of possession of the said premises shall pay to the Promoter such proportionate share of the outgoings as may be determined by the Promoter and which are not covered in any other provisions of this agreement.

11. The Allottee shall pay to the Promoter a sum of Rs. .... for meeting all legal costs, charges and expenses, including professional costs of the Attorney-at-Law/Advocates of the Promoter in connection with formation of the said Society, or Limited Company, or Apex Body or Federation and for preparing its rules, regulations and bye-laws and the cost of preparing and engrossing the conveyance or assignment of lease.

12. At the time of registration of conveyance or Lease of the structure of the building or wing of the building, the Allottee shall pay to the Promoter, the Allottees' share of stamp duty and registration charges payable, by the said Society or Limited Company on such conveyance or lease or any

document or instrument of transfer in respect of the structure of the said Building /wing of the building. At the time of registration of conveyance or Lease of the project land, the Allottee shall pay to the Promoter, the Allottees' share of stamp duty and registration charges payable, by the said Apex Body or Federation on such conveyance or lease or any document or instrument of transfer in respect of the structure of the said land to be executed in favour of the Apex Body or Federation.

13. REPRESENTATIONS AND WARRANTIES OF THE PROMOTER
    The Promoter hereby represents and warrants to the Allottee as follows:

    i. The Promoter has clear and marketable title with respect to the project land; as declared in the title report annexed to this agreement and has the requisite rights to carry out development upon the project land and also has actual, physical and legal possession of the project land for the implementation of the Project;
    ii. The Promoter has lawful rights and requisite approvals from the competent Authorities to carry out development of the Project and shall obtain requisite approvals from time to time to complete the development of the project;
    iii. There are no encumbrances upon the project land or the Project except those disclosed in the title report;
    iv. There are no litigations pending before any Court of law with respect to the project land or Project except those disclosed in the title report;
    v. All approvals, licenses and permits issued by the competent authorities with respect to the Project, project land and said building/wing are valid and subsisting and have been obtained by following due process of law. Further, all approvals, licenses and permits to be issued by the competent authorities with respect to the Project, project land and said building/wing shall be obtained by following due process of law and the Promoter has been and shall, at all times, remain to be in compliance with all applicable laws in relation to the Project, project land, Building/wing and common areas;
    vi. The Promoter has the right to enter into this Agreement and has not committed or omitted to perform any act or thing, whereby the right, title and interest of the Allottee created herein, may prejudicially be affected;
    vii. The Promoter has not entered into any agreement for sale and/or development agreement or any other agreement / arrangement with any person or party with respect to the project land, including the Project and the said [Apartment/Plot] which will, in any manner, affect the rights of Allottee under this Agreement;
    viii. The Promoter confirms that the Promoter is not restricted in any manner whatsoever from selling the said [Apartment/Plot] to the Allottee in the manner contemplated in this Agreement;
    ix. At the time of execution of the conveyance deed of the structure to the association of allottees the Promoter shall handover lawful, vacant, peaceful, physical possession of the common areas of the Structure to the Association of the Allottees;
    x. The Promoter has duly paid and shall continue to pay and discharge undisputed governmental dues, rates, charges and taxes and other monies, levies, impositions, premiums, damages and/or penalties and other outgoings, whatsoever, payable with respect to the said project to the competent Authorities;
    xi. No notice from the Government or any other local body or authority or any legislative enactment, government ordinance, order, notification (including any notice for acquisition or requisition of the said property) has been received or served upon the Promoter in respect of the project land and/or the Project except those disclosed in the title report.

14. The Allottee/s or himself/themselves with intention to bring all persons into whosoever hands the Apartment may come, hereby covenants with the Promoter as follows :-
    i. To maintain the Apartment at the Allottee's own cost in good and tenantable repair and condition from the date that of possession of the Apartment is taken and shall not do or suffer to be done anything in or to the building in which the Apartment is situated which may be against the rules, regulations or bye-laws or change/alter or make addition in or to the building in which the Apartment is situated and the Apartment itself or any part thereof without the consent of the local authorities, if required.
    ii. Not to store in the Apartment any goods which are of hazardous, combustible or dangerous nature or are so heavy as to damage the construction or structure of the building in which the Apartment is situated or storing of which goods is objected to by the concerned local or other authority and shall take care while carrying heavy packages which may damage or likely to damage the staircases, common passages or any other structure of the building in which the Apartment is situated, including entrances of the building in which the Apartment is situated and in case any damage is caused to the building in which the Apartment is situated or the Apartment on account of negligence or default of the Allottee in this behalf, the Allottee shall be liable for the consequences of the breach.
    iii. To carry out at his own cost all internal repairs to the said Apartment and maintain the Apartment in the same condition, state and order in which it was delivered by the Promoter to the Allottee and shall not do or suffer to be done anything in or to the building in which the Apartment is situated or the Apartment which may be contrary to the rules and regulations and bye-laws of the concerned local authority or other public authority. In the event of the Allottee committing any act in contravention of the above provision, the Allottee shall be responsible and liable for the consequences thereof to the concerned local authority and/or other public authority.
    iv. Not to demolish or cause to be demolished the Apartment or any part thereof, nor at any time make or cause to be made any addition or alteration of whatever nature in or to the Apartment or any part thereof, nor any alteration in the elevation and outside colour scheme of the building in which the Apartment is situated and shall keep the portion, sewers, drains and pipes in the Apartment and the appurtenances thereto in good tenantable repair and condition, and in particular, so as to support shelter and protect the other parts of the building in which the Apartment is situated and shall not chisel or in any other manner cause damage to columns, beams, walls, slabs or RCC, Pardis or other structural members in the Apartment without the prior written permission of the Promoter and/or the Society or the Limited Company.
    v. Not to do or permit to be done any act or thing which may render void or voidable any insurance of the project land and the building in which the Apartment is situated or any part thereof or whereby any increased premium shall become payable in respect of the insurance.
    vi. Not to throw dirt, rubbish, rags, garbage or other refuse or permit the same to be thrown from the said Apartment in the compound or any portion of the project land and the building in which the Apartment is situated.
    vii. Pay to the Promoter within fifteen days of demand by the Promoter, his share of security deposit demanded by the concerned local authority or Government or giving water, electricity or any other service connection to the building in which the Apartment is situated.

viii. To bear and pay increase in local taxes, water charges, insurance and such other levies, if any, which are imposed by the concerned local authority and/or Government and/or other public authority, on account of change of user of the Apartment by the Allottee for any purposes other than for purpose for which it is sold.

ix. The Allottee shall not let, sub-let, transfer, assign or part with interest or benefit factor of this Agreement or part with the possession of the Apartment until all the dues payable by the Allottee to the Promoter under this Agreement are fully paid up.

x. The Allottee shall observe and perform all the rules and regulations which the Society or the Limited Company or Apex Body or Federation may adopt at its inception and the additions, alterations or amendments thereof that may be made from time to time for protection and maintenance of the said building and the Apartments therein and for the observance and performance of the Building Rules, Regulations and Bye-laws for the time being of the concerned local authority and of Government and other public bodies. The Allottee shall also observe and perform all the stipulations and conditions laid down by the Society/Limited Company/Apex Body/Federation regarding the occupancy and use of the Apartment in the Building and shall pay and contribute regularly and punctually towards the taxes, expenses or other out-goings in accordance with the terms of this Agreement.

xi. The Allottee shall permit the Promoter and their surveyors and agents, with or without workmen and others, at all reasonable times, to enter into and upon the said buildings or any part thereof to view and examine the state and condition thereof.

xii. The Allottee shall permit the Promoter and their surveyors and agents, with or without workmen and others, at all reasonable times, to enter into and upon the project land or any part thereof to view and examine the state and condition thereof.

15. The Promoter shall maintain a separate account in respect of sums received by the Promoter from the Allottee as advance or deposit, sums received on account of the share capital for the promotion of the Co-operative Society or association or Company or towards the out goings, legal charges and shall utilize the amounts only for the purposes for which they have been received.

16. Nothing contained in this Agreement is intended to be nor shall be construed as a grant, demise or assignment in law, of the said Apartments or of the said Plot and Building or any part thereof. The Allottee shall have no claim save and except in respect of the Apartment hereby agreed to be sold to him and all open spaces, parking spaces, lobbies, staircases, terraces recreation spaces, will remain the property of the Promoter until the same is transferred as hereinbefore mentioned.

17. PROMOTER SHALL NOT MORTGAGE OR CREATE A CHARGE
After the Promoter executes this Agreement he shall not mortgage or create a charge on the *[Apartment/] and if any such mortgage or charge is made or created then notwithstanding anything contained in any other law for the time being in force, such mortgage or charge shall not affect the right and interest of the Allottee who has taken or agreed to take such [Apartment/plot].

18. BINDING EFFECT
Forwarding this Agreement to the Allottee by the Promoter does not create a binding obligation on the part of the Promoter or the Allottee until, firstly, the Allottee signs and delivers this Agreement with all the schedules along with the payments due as stipulated in the Payment Plan within 30 (thirty) days from the date of receipt by the Allottee and secondly, appears for registration of the same before the concerned Sub-Registrar as and when intimated by the Promoter. If the

Allottee(s) fails to execute and deliver to the Promoter this Agreement within 30 (thirty) days from the date of its receipt by the Allottee and/or appear before the Sub-Registrar for its registration as and when intimated by the Promoter, then the Promoter shall serve a notice to the Allottee for rectifying the default, which if not rectified within 15 (fifteen) days from the date of its receipt by the Allottee, application of the Allottee shall be treated as cancelled and all sums deposited by the Allottee in connection therewith including the booking amount shall be returned to the Allottee without any interest or compensation whatsoever.

19. ENTIRE AGREEMENT

This Agreement, along with its schedules and annexures, constitutes the entire Agreement between the Parties with respect to the subject matter hereof and supersedes any and all understandings, any other agreements, allotment letter, correspondences, arrangements whether written or oral, if any, between the Parties in regard to the said apartment/plot/building, as the case may be.

20. RIGHT TO AMEND

This Agreement may only be amended through written consent of the Parties.

21. PROVISIONS OF THIS AGREEMENT APPLICABLE TO ALLOTTEE/ SUBSEQUENT ALLOTTEES

It is clearly understood and so agreed by and between the Parties hereto that all the provisions contained herein and the obligations arising hereunder in respect of the Project shall equally be applicable to and enforceable against any subsequent Allottees of the [Apartment/Plot], in case of a transfer, as the said obligations go along with the [Apartment/Plot] for all intents and purposes.

22. SEVERABILITY

If any provision of this Agreement shall be determined to be void or unenforceable under the Act or the Rules and Regulations made thereunder or under other applicable laws, such provisions of the Agreement shall be deemed amended or deleted in so far as reasonably inconsistent with the purpose of this Agreement and to the extent necessary to conform to Act or the Rules and Regulations made thereunder or the applicable law, as the case may be, and the remaining provisions of this Agreement shall remain valid and enforceable as applicable at the time of execution of this Agreement.

23. METHOD OF CALCULATION OF PROPORTIONATE SHARE WHEREVER REFERRED TO IN THE AGREEMENT

Wherever in this Agreement it is stipulated that the Allottee has to make any payment, in common with other Allottee(s) in Project, the same shall be in proportion to the carpet area of the [Apartment/Plot] to the total carpet area of all the [Apartments/Plots] in the Project.

24. FURTHER ASSURANCES

Both Parties agree that they shall execute, acknowledge and deliver to the other such instruments and take such other actions, in additions to the instruments and actions specifically provided for herein, as may be reasonably required in order to effectuate the provisions of this Agreement or of any transaction contemplated herein or to confirm or perfect any right to be created or transferred hereunder or pursuant to any such transaction.

25. PLACE OF EXECUTION

The execution of this Agreement shall be complete only upon its execution by the Promoter through its authorized signatory at the Promoter's Office, or at some other place, which may be mutually agreed between the Promoter and the Allottee, in _____ after the Agreement is duly executed by the Allottee and the Promoter or simultaneously with the execution the said Agreement shall be registered at the office of the Sub-Registrar. Hence this Agreement shall be deemed to have been executed at_____.

26. The Allottee and/or Promoter shall present this Agreement as well as the conveyance/assignment of lease at the proper registration office of registration within the time limit prescribed by the Registration Act and the Promoter will attend such office and admit execution thereof.

27. That all notices to be served on the Allottee and the Promoter as contemplated by this Agreement shall be deemed to have been duly served if sent to the Allottee or the Promoter by Registered Post A.D and notified Email ID/Under Certificate of Posting at their respective addresses specified below:

_____Name of Allottee
_____(Allottee's Address) Notified Email ID:_____

M/s_____Promoter name
_____(Promoter Address) Notified Email ID: _____

It shall be the duty of the Allottee and the promoter to inform each other of any change in address subsequent to the execution of this Agreement in the above address by Registered Post failing which all communications and letters posted at the above address shall be deemed to have been received by the promoter or the Allottee, as the case may be.

28. JOINT ALLOTTEES
That in case there are Joint Allottees all communications shall be sent by the Promoter to the Allottee whose name appears first and at the address given by him/her which shall for all intents and purposes to consider as properly served on all the Allottees.

29. Stamp Duty and Registration:- The charges towards stamp duty and Registration of this Agreement shall be borne by the allottee.

30. Dispute Resolution:- Any dispute between parties shall be settled amicably. In case of failure to settled the dispute amicably, which shall be referred to the _____ Authority as per the provisions of the Real Estate (Regulation and Development) Act, 2016, Rules and Regulations, thereunder.

31. GOVERNING LAW
That the rights and obligations of the parties under or arising out of this Agreement shall be construed and enforced in accordance with the laws of India for the time being in force and the _____ courts will have the jurisdiction for this Agreement

IN WITNESS WHEREOF parties hereinabove named have set their respective hands and signed this Agreement for sale at_____*(city/town name)* in the presence of attesting witness, signing as such on the day first above written.

First Schedule Above Referred to Description of the freehold/leasehold land and all other details.

Second Schedule Above Referred to here set out the nature, extent and description of common areas and facilities.

SIGNED AND DELIVERED BY THE WITHIN NAMED

Allottee: (including joint buyers)

Please affix photograph and sign across the photograph	Please affix photograph and sign across the photograph

(1)_____

(2)_____

At_____on_____

in the presence of WITNESSES:

1.   Name _____
     Signature _____

2.   Name _____
     Signature _____

_____

SIGNED AND DELIVERED BY THE WITHIN NAMED

Promoter:

(1)_____

(Authorized Signatory) WITNESSES:

| Please affix photograph and sign across the photograp |

Name _____
Signature _____

Name _____
Signature _____

Note – Execution clauses to be finalised in individual cases having regard to the constitution of the parties to the Agreement.

SCHEDULE 'A'

PLEASE INSERT DESCRIPTION OF THE [APARTMENT/PLOT] AND THE GARAGE/CLOSED PARKING (IF APPLICABLE) ALONG WITH BOUNDARIES IN ALL FOUR DIRECTIONS

SCHEDULE 'B'
FLOOR PLAN OF THE APARTMENT

ANNEXURE -A
(Authenticated copies of the plans and specifications of the Apartment agreed to be purchased by the Allottee as approved by the concerned local authority)

ANNEXURE –B
(Authenticated copy of the Registration Certificate of the Project granted by the Real Estate Regulatory Authority)

ANNEXURE – C
(Specification and amenities for the Apartment)

Received of and from the Allottee above named the sum of Rupees .... on execution of this agreement towards Earnest Money Deposit or application fee I say received.

The Promoter/s.

www.ingramcontent.com/pod-product-compliance
Lightning Source LLC
Chambersburg PA
CBHW062104220526
45471CB00010B/3597